A WORLD OF DOLLS
THAT YOU CAN MAKE

ALSO BY LYNN EDELMAN SCHNURNBERGER
Kings, Queens, Knights & Jesters

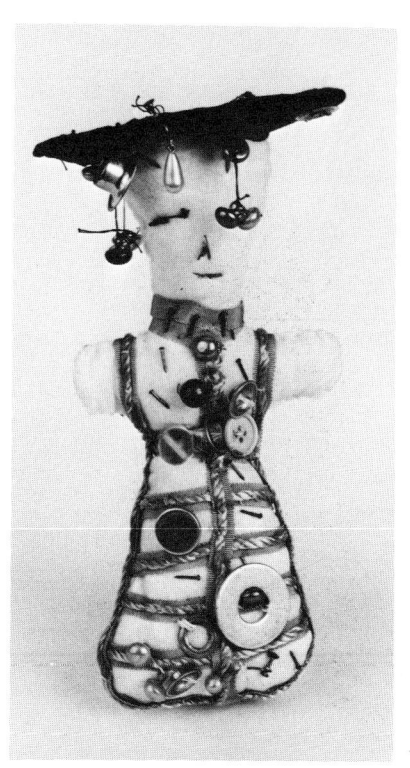

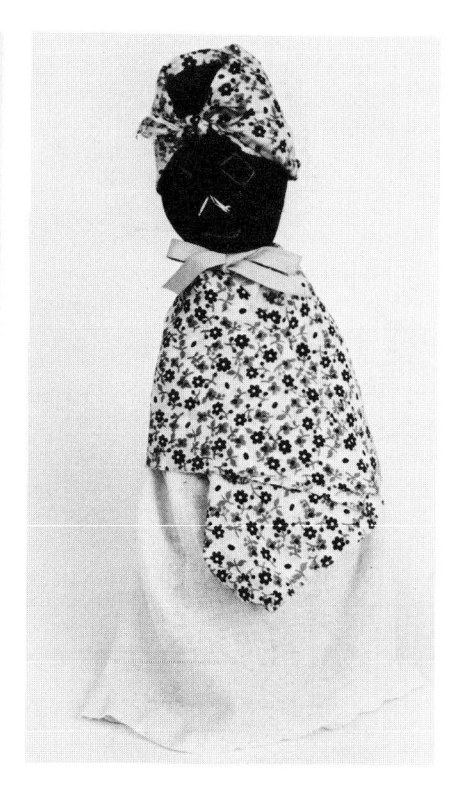

A WORLD OF
DOLLS
THAT YOU CAN MAKE

LYNN EDELMAN SCHNURNBERGER
photographs by Barbara Brooks
drawings by Alan Robert Showe

1 8 17
HARPER & ROW, PUBLISHERS
Cambridge, Philadelphia, San Francisco, London, Mexico City, São Paulo, Sydney
NEW YORK

A World of Dolls That You Can Make

Text copyright © 1982 by Lynn Edelman Schnurnberger
Photographs copyright © 1982 by Barbara Brooks
Drawings copyright © 1982 by Alan Robert Showe

All rights reserved. No part of this book may be used or reproduced in any manner whatsoever without written permission except in the case of brief quotations embodied in critical articles and reviews. Printed in the United States of America. For information address Harper & Row, Publishers, Inc., 10 East 53rd Street, New York, N.Y. 10022. Published simultaneously in Canada by Fitzhenry & Whiteside Limited, Toronto.

First Edition

Library of Congress Cataloging in Publication Data
Schnurnberger, Lynn Edelman.
  A world of dolls.

  Summary: Presents the historical background of and simple instructions for fourteen easy-to-make dolls from various times and cultures.
   1. Dollmaking—Juvenile literature.   2. Doll clothes—Juvenile literature.   [1. Dollmaking. 2. Dolls]   I. Brooks, Barbara, ill.   II. Showe, Alan Robert, ill.   III. Title.
TT175.S36   1982   745.592'21   80-8450
ISBN 0-06-025231-6   AACR2
ISBN 0-06-025232-4 (lib. bdg.)

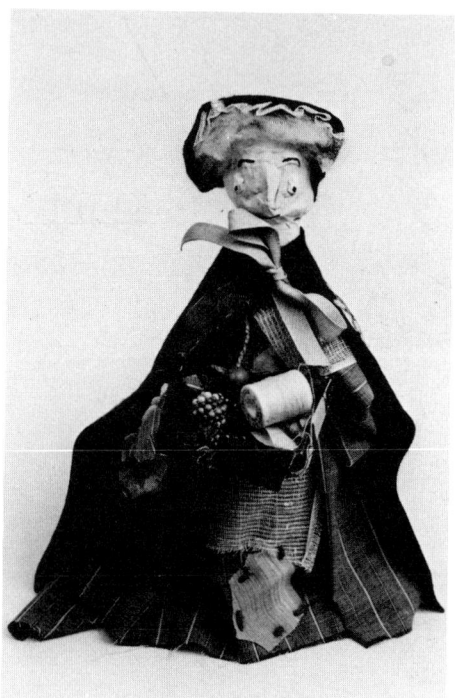

ACKNOWLEDGMENTS

The production of a book requires the help and advice of a whole team of behind-the-scenes people. My thanks to Elizabeth Gordon, Jane Feder, and Teresa Moogan at Harper & Row, for their suggestions and work on the manuscript.

To Renée Cafiero, who copyedited the book, and to Ellen Weiss, who designed it.

To some not so behind-the-scenes people—Shelia Basden, Vincent Bernard, Lourdes Diaz, Wilma Diaz, Molly Eagen, Lori Edelman, Peter Gee, Donna Harkavy, John Herbst, Erica Hutchinson, Joo Hee Kim, Monica Kim, Ben Mandel, Rachel Mason, Jillian Risberg, Molla Risberg, Charles Robinson, Elizabeth Sanchez, Juan Sanchez, Alan Showe, Amy Tarr, and Jerome Whitehurst, who modeled for the photographs.

To Nancy Paine of the Brooklyn Children's Museum, and the curators and librarians at all of the institutions from which pictures of dolls were selected, for sharing their expertise and pointing me in the direction of interesting photographs.

To my family and friends, for their continuing interest and patience.

And to The Writer's Room—a very special workplace in New York City where this book was written.

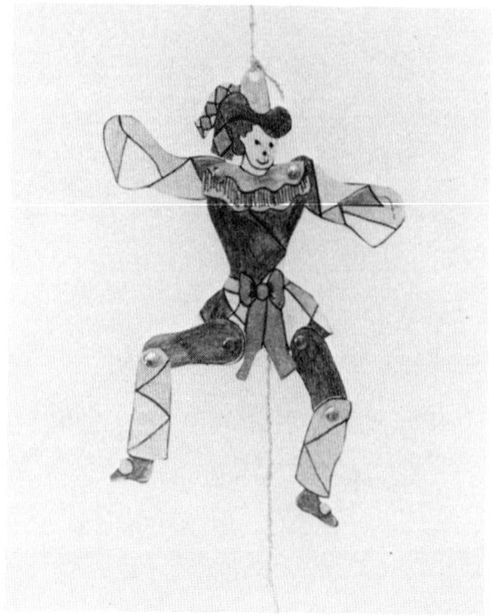

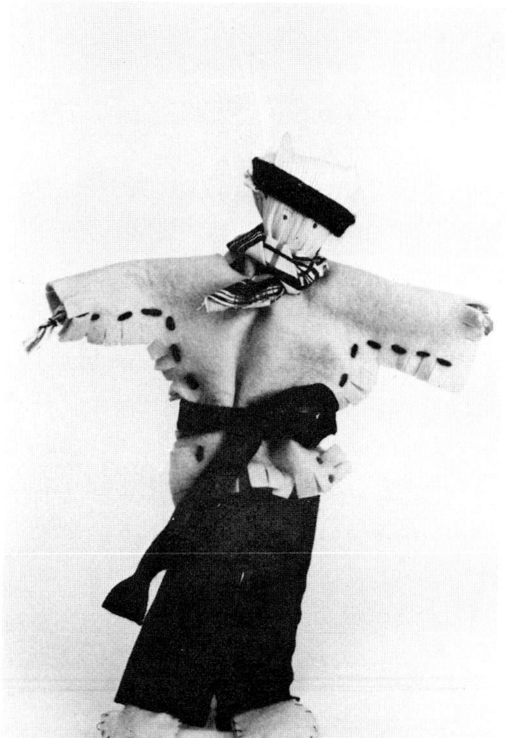

CONTENTS

Introduction	ix
Supplies and Directions	1
The Dolls	13
Czechoslovakian Doll	14
Rag Doll	18
Rag Broom Doll	26
Colima Clay Doll	30
Turkish Sock Doll	34
Indian Cornhusk Dolls	42
Iroquois Cornhusk Doll	44
Odas	50
Pantin	54
Peddler Doll	58
Peruvian Doll	68
Zulu Doll	74
Kachina Butterfly Maiden	80
Sudanese Bride Doll	84
Fortune-Telling Doll	88
The Patterns	97

*Courtesy Museum of
the City of New York*

INTRODUCTION

Paper dolls and patchwork dolls, Kewpie dolls and Snoopy dolls. Dolls to look at, play with, talk to—whether you have one or many, dolls are treasured friends.

As far back as the ancient Egyptians, who fashioned dolls out of cloth, people have had dolls. The Egyptians made them for their children to play with, but sometimes people made dolls for other reasons. In Britain, people made lifesize "kern babies," corn dolls dressed up in women's clothing, which they used to celebrate the harvest. In eighteenth-century France, before there were fashion magazines, designers dressed dolls in miniature copies of their latest creations and mailed them to America, to advertise new styles of clothing. There are dolls that are used for magic and dolls that are worshiped as idols. Sometimes we don't know exactly the reason dolls were made, but most dolls tell us something about the people who made them. For instance, a doll's clothing can tell us how people dressed.

Almost anything can be a doll. It can be as simple as a twig, with branches for arms and legs, that you dance around on your knee. In Africa children play with bone dolls, and early American settlers painted faces on cornhusks and wrapped them up in small blankets.

The Greek word for doll, "kore," means girl. In Sanskrit, the ancient language of India, dolls are "puttelis," or little daughters. And in Western Europe dolls used to be called "little ladies." But not all dolls are replicas of girls or women. Many dolls, like tin soldiers, today's popular Ken doll, or the Turkish doll illustrated in this book, are male.

People usually make dolls out of materials that are easy to get. Often they use what they find growing around them. In Indonesia, where there are lots of trees, people make wood dolls. In other places dolls are made from flowers and grass. Foods are fashioned into dolls—for example, where they are plentiful, apples, nuts, and prunes all are made into dolls. Many dolls are made from materials found around the house: Clothespins, hankies, and scraps of fabric have all been used to make dolls.

The fourteen dolls in this book are based on historical dolls. They were made in different parts of the world, in different centuries, and they hint at the wide variety of materials that have been used by various doll makers. There is a doll made out of clay, one made out of paper, and even a doll made out of an old broom. Some of the materials are not as easy for us to obtain as they were for the people who created these dolls. Since the original doll makers used what was handy, the instructions in this book sometimes call for materials which, though different from the originals, are readily available today.

All of these dolls were handmade; that means that no two dolls of the same type looked exactly alike. This book will show you pictures of dolls and give the basic instructions for making them, but there are parts of each doll, or the doll's costume, where you can add your own individual touch. The ribbons and fabrics you use, the faces you paint on the dolls, the designs you paint on their clothing, the buttons, beads, and accessories you add, will make each doll you create uniquely your own. That's what's special about a doll you make—there's no other doll like it in the whole world.

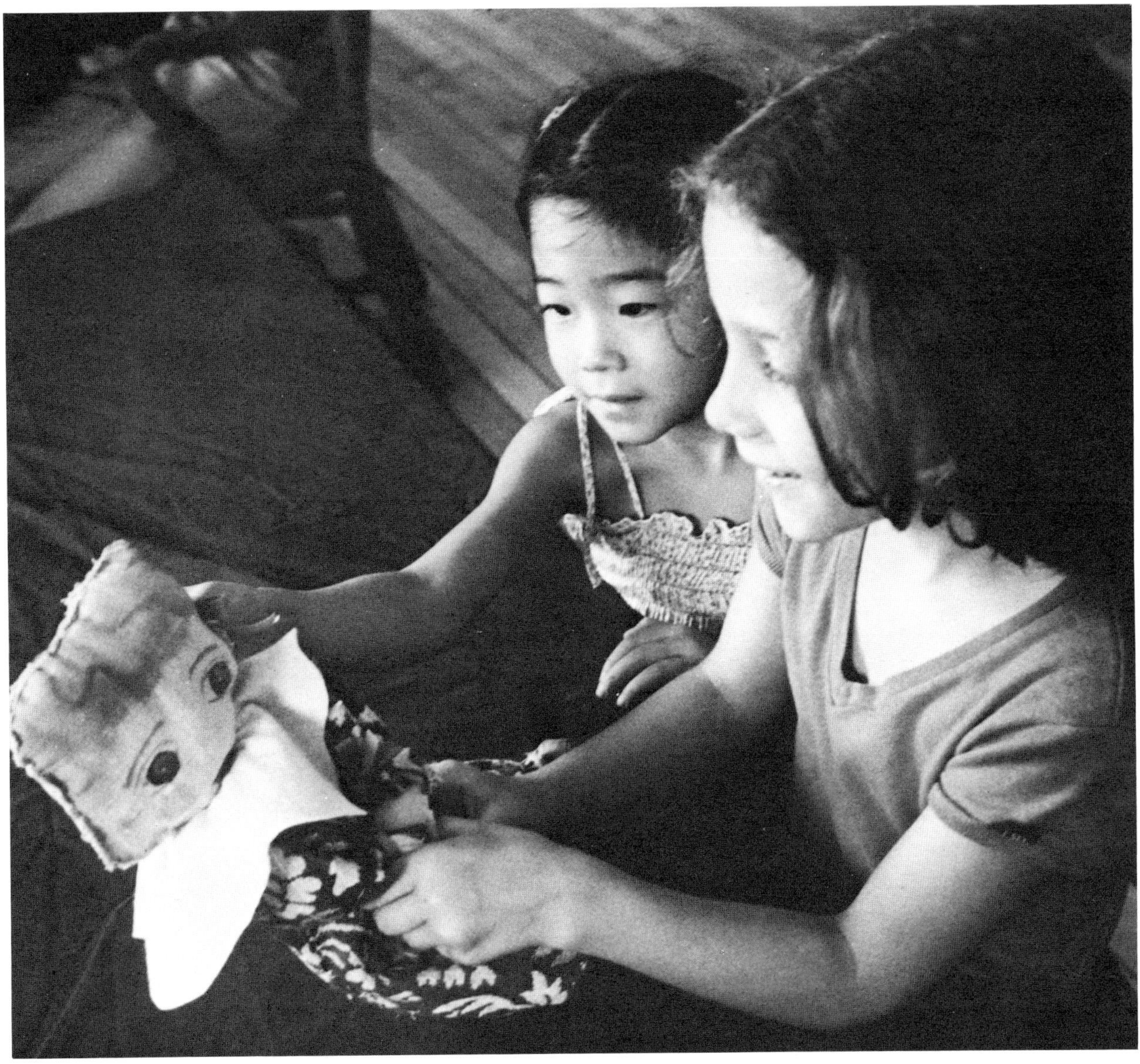

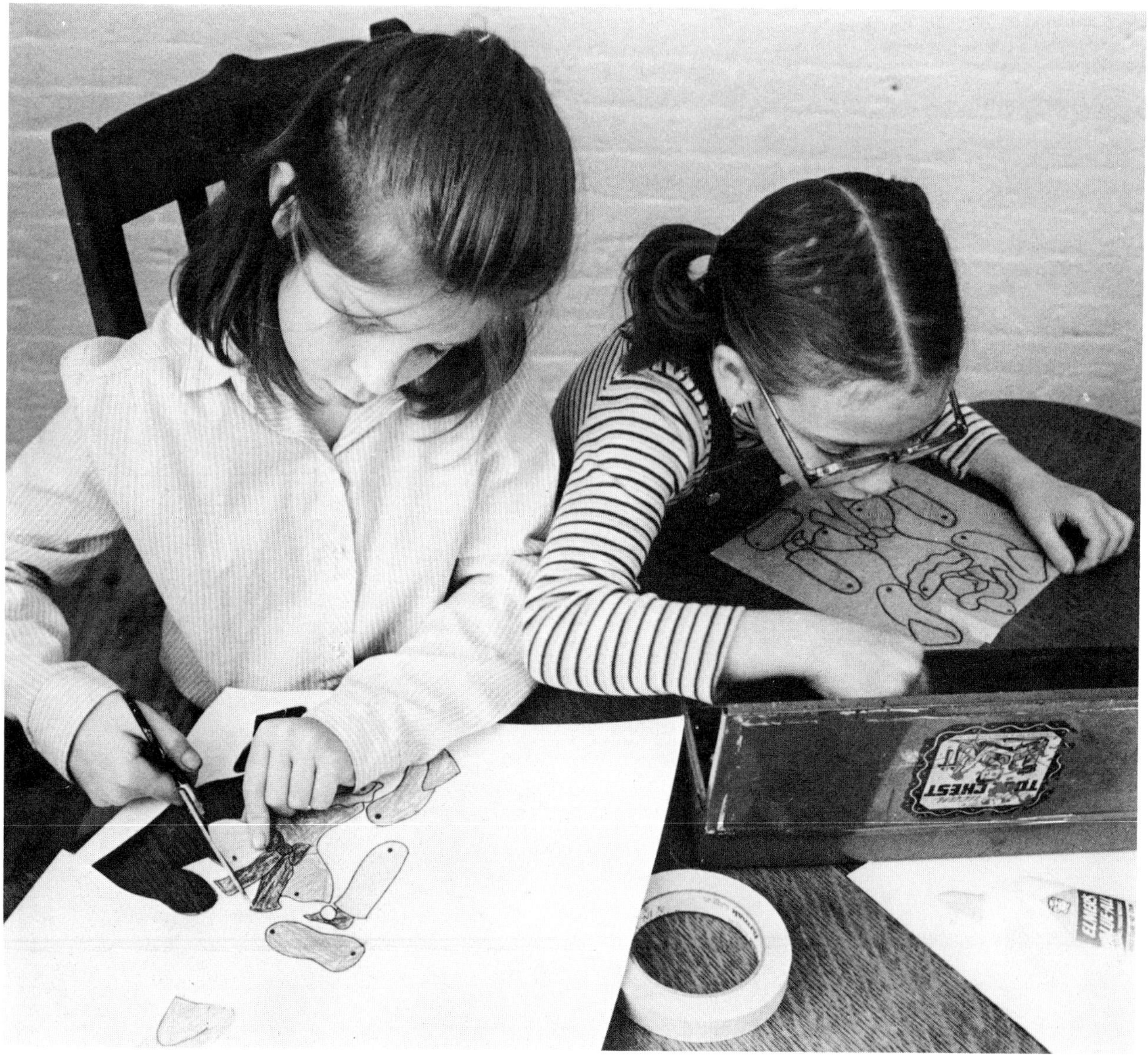
TOY CHEST

SUPPLIES AND DIRECTIONS

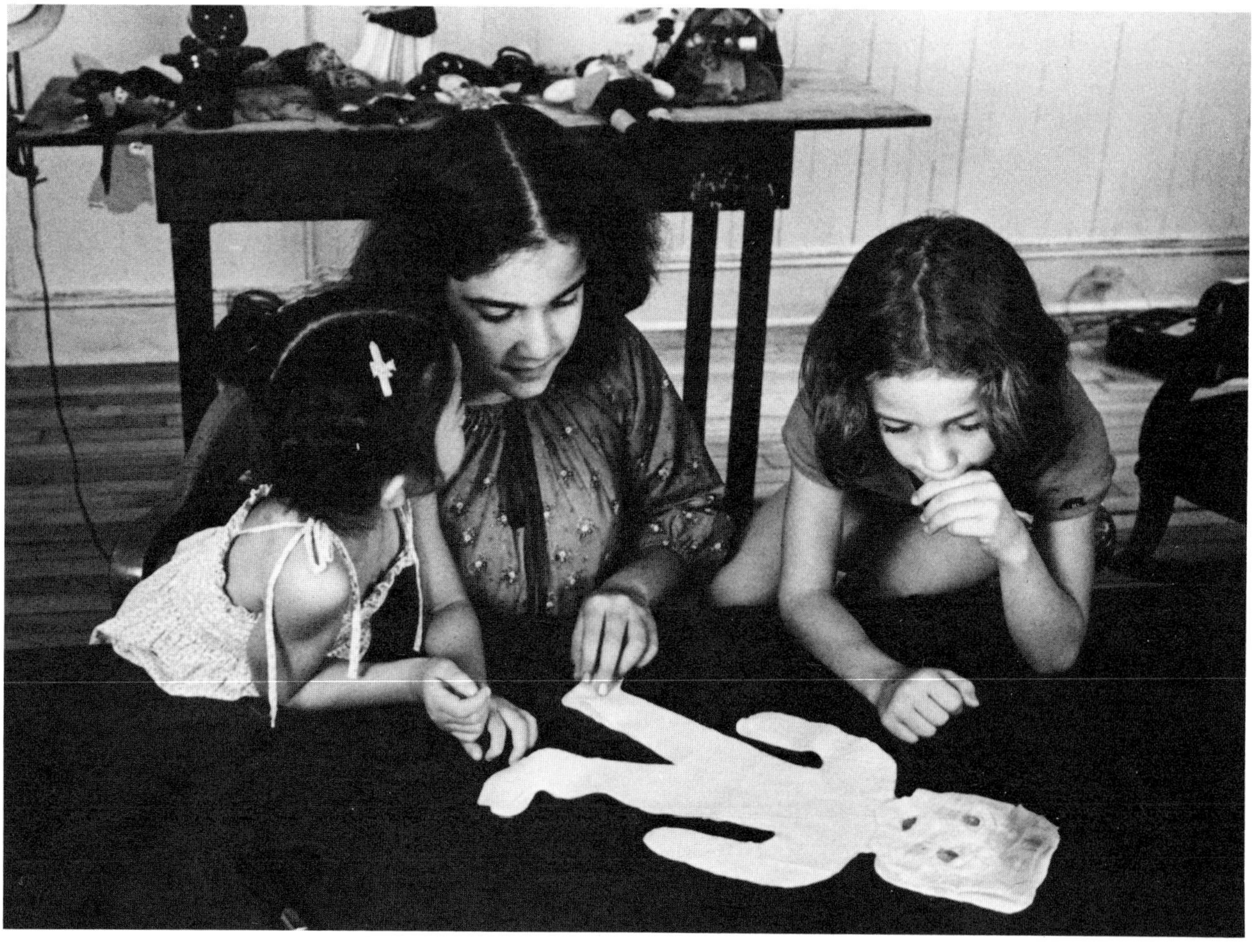

SUPPLIES AND DIRECTIONS

Before you make any doll, read through the instructions carefully. There will be a list of all the things you need to make the doll. Common, everyday items, like scissors and tape, will be listed first, as *General Supplies.* These will be followed by a list and description of special items, like fabric or beads, that you need to assemble for a particular doll. Have all of your supplies on hand before you start working.

Unless there are specific instructions, you can make all of the dolls using everyday sewing and craft skills. The following are descriptions of a few supplies and explanations of the special craft techniques that will be called for throughout the book.

Fabric:
Sometimes a certain kind of fabric, like cotton or felt, is recommended. Otherwise, you can use whatever kind of fabric you want. Most of the dolls and their costumes don't require very large pieces of fabric, and you might find just what you're looking for around your house—perhaps an old sheet or pillowcase, fabric left over from another sewing project, or a swatch of material salvaged from a worn-out piece of clothing. Felt is the easiest fabric to work with because the edges don't unravel when you cut it. If you use any other kind of fabric, iron down the edges before you sew the doll or the costume together.

Scraps of Fabric to Stuff a Doll:

You can use leftover scraps of fabric, or wads of regular household cotton to stuff dolls. You can also use foam rubber, gauze, or cotton batting. Almost any soft material will do. Foam rubber and cotton batting can be purchased at most sewing stores.

Overcast Stitch:

An overcast stitch is used to join two pieces of fabric together.

1. Place one piece of fabric directly on top of the other and line up the edges.

Starting at one end of the fabric, push your threaded needle up from underneath, through both pieces of fabric, about ¼ inch in from the edge.

2. Pull the threaded needle around again to the underside of the double layer of fabric, about ¼ inch from the first stitch along the edge. Repeat this edging until the two pieces are sewn together,

3. and then tie the thread off with a knot.

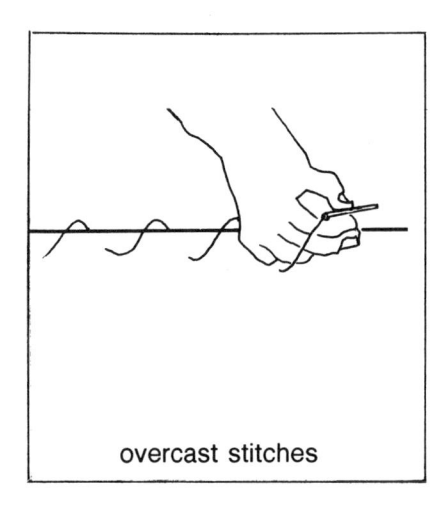

overcast stitches

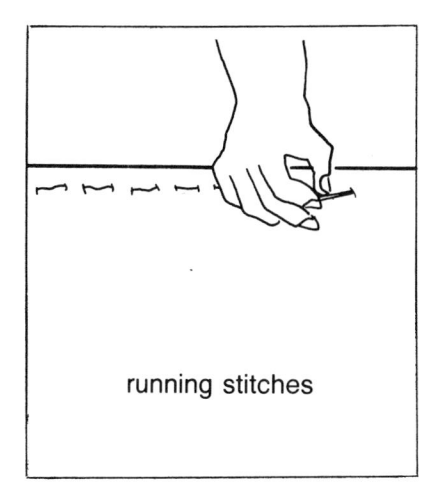

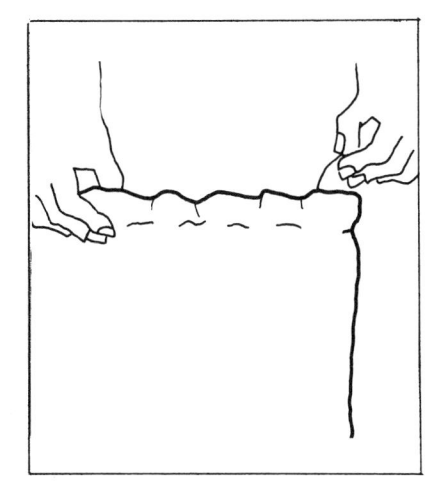

Gather with a Running Stitch:

A quick way of stringing a piece of fabric on a thread is to gather it with a running stitch.

1. Put the threaded needle down through one side of the fabric at one corner and up through the other side about an inch away along the edge. Use this weaving motion in and out at about 1-inch intervals in a straight line along the entire edge of the fabric.

2. Then scrunch the fabric together by pulling the thread and needle until the material is gathered to the length you need.

3. Tie the end of the thread off with a knot.

Sometimes, after a costume is on a doll, the instructions will tell you to use a running stitch to gather a neckline or a sleeve to hold the costume in place.

1. Weave a threaded needle in and out around the edge of the neckline or sleeve,

2. pull the thread tightly, scrunching the fabric together,

3. and then tie the thread off with a knot.

running stitches

Fold the Fabric into Quarters:

This direction allows you to make the front and the back of a costume out of one piece of fabric.

1. Lay out the fabric with the short sides at the top and bottom.

2. Fold the fabric in half from top to bottom,

3. and in half again from left to right. This second fold in the fabric should be on the left side.

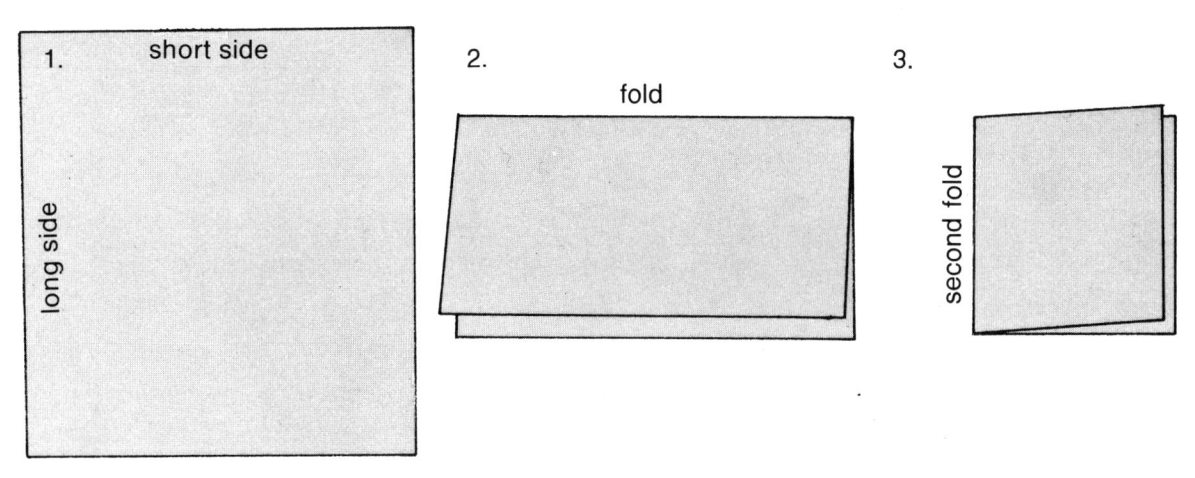

Measure and Cut a Neckline:

When you measure and cut a neckline, you cut a circle out of the middle of a piece of fabric so you can put the costume on over the doll's head.

1. Fold the fabric into quarters, as just shown.

2. Place a ruler along the fold on the left side. The zero should be in the upper left corner. Measure along this line and use a pencil to mark off the number of inches called for by the instructions.

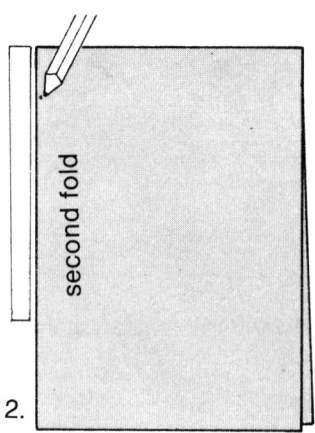

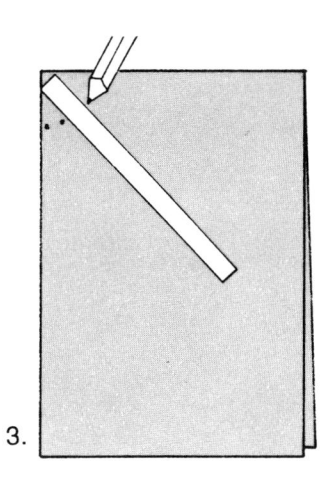

3. Keeping the zero in the upper left corner, move the ruler in an arc across the fabric. Measure and mark off the same number of inches in several places, including the top fold.

4. Connect these points with a curved pencil line.

5. Cut along this line,

6. through all four layers of fabric.

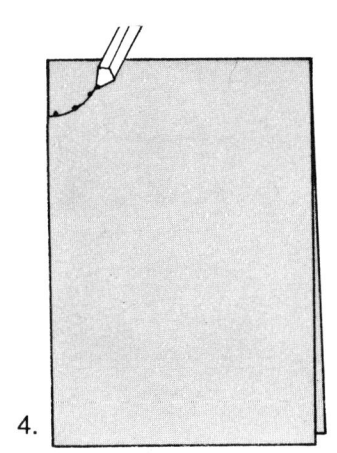

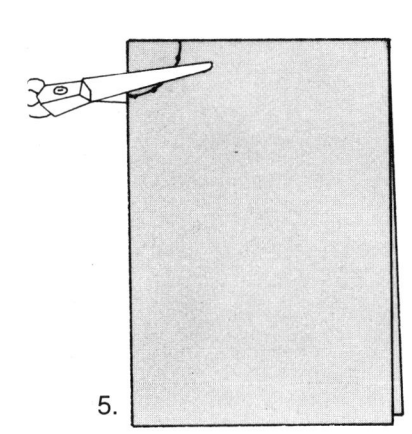

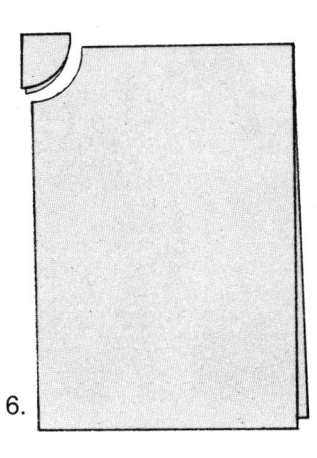

Papier-Mâché:

Papier-mâché is a kind of surface covering made of paper and glue. It makes the surface hard and solid.

To make papier-mâché you will need a bowl, newspapers, and a glue made from water and wallpaper paste or flour. Wallpaper paste can be purchased at a hardware store.

1. Mix the glue: Pour about 1 cup of wallpaper paste or flour into the bowl and slowly add water. Use about 3 times as much water as you do wallpaper paste or flour. Mix it with your hands to get out the lumps. It will feel sticky. Keep adding water and mixing it until the glue has the consistency of oatmeal.

2. Tear—do not cut—the newspaper into pieces about 3 inches square.

3. Spread the glue on the newspaper. Don't dunk the pieces, because you will end up with too much glue on the newspaper and it will be messy and hard to handle.

4. Put the gluey newspaper on the area you want to cover. Overlap the pieces of newspaper slightly at the edges, so you get a flat surface. Wipe off any extra glue. Always wait until the papier-mâché is completely dry, about 24 hours, before you paint or decorate it.

Make a Tracing-Paper Pattern:

There are over 20 patterns for dolls and dolls' clothes in this book. To use them without cutting up the book, you can make a tracing-paper pattern. You will need a pencil, white chalk, a ruler, scissors, tracing paper, carbon paper, straight pins, and masking tape.

1. Use a piece of tracing paper a little bit bigger than the pattern you want to trace. Tape the tracing paper over the printed pattern.

2. Trace around the pattern with the pencil. Be sure to trace any dots, lines, or labels just the way they appear on the pattern. Use a ruler or straight edge to help trace over straight lines.

3. Gently unstick the tape and cut out the tracing-paper pattern.

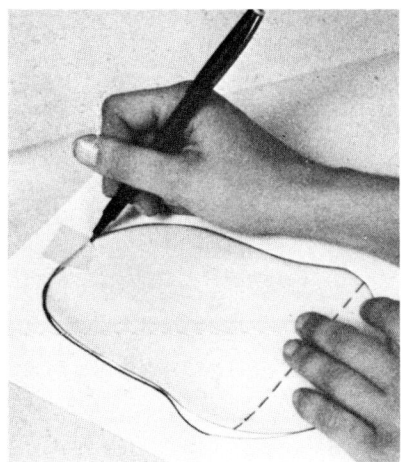

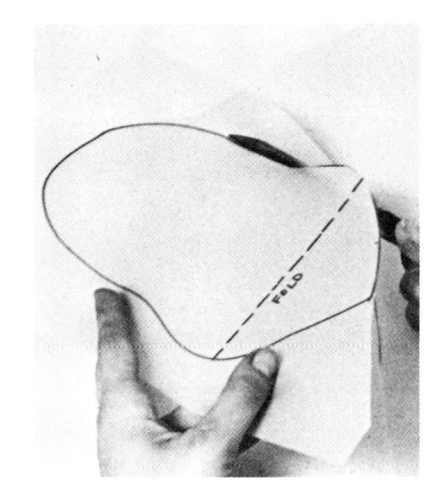

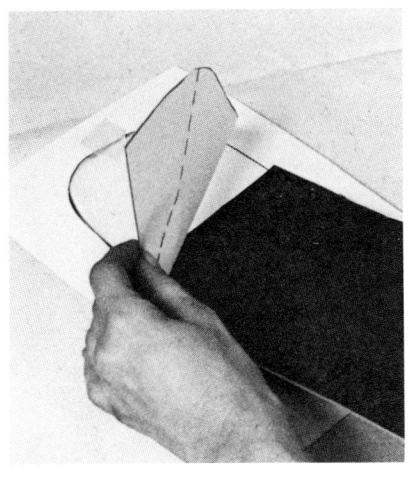

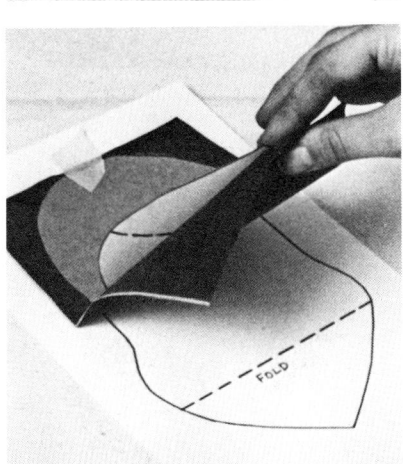

4. To trace the pattern onto paper, tape the pattern to the paper. To trace it onto fabric, use straight pins and pin the pattern to the fabric. If the instructions call for you to trace the pattern shape more than once on a single piece of paper or fabric, be sure to leave enough room to do so.

5. Trace around the pattern. Again, use a ruler or straight edge where there are straight lines. If you are using a dark-colored material, use chalk to trace around the pattern; otherwise use a pencil.

After you have traced around the pattern, hold the pattern down with your hand and gently remove the tape. Trace around those areas in the outline that the tape covered.

6. To transfer dots or broken lines to fabric or paper, put a piece of carbon paper, with the shiny, carbon side down, between the tracing-paper pattern and the fabric or paper.

7. Use a pencil and trace over the dots and broken lines. You do not have to trace labels. The labels are there to help you identify things in the instructions, so just keep the pattern handy while you're working.

8. Untape or unpin the pattern. Remove the tracing and carbon papers.

9. Carefully cut out the material along the traced pencil line.

11

12

THE DOLLS

CZECHOSLOVAKIAN DOLL

*Courtesy Brooklyn
Children's Museum*

Czechoslovakian doll makers carved just two simple wooden shapes—a ball and a cone—painted them with bright poster-paint colors, and made these tiny costume dolls for children to play with. They're only 5 inches high, but they show us native Czechoslovakian dress—costumes that are no longer worn today, but were once worn by milkmaids or shepherdesses as they went about their work.

Costume dolls—whether elaborately dressed Spanish dancers in satin ruffles and rhinestone tiaras or Czechoslovakian peasant girls in caps and aprons—help us imagine what it might be like to live in another country, or even in a different century.

Often, Czech children had two or three of these dolls, displayed on a shelf. They're so easy you can make several Czechoslovakian peasant dolls at the same time.

General Supplies:

A pencil, masking tape, paint, and a paintbrush.

To make each doll, use a Styrofoam ball 2 to 3 inches in diameter for the head, and a Styrofoam cone 4 inches high for the body. Styrofoam can be purchased in art stores, craft supply stores, and some five-and-tens. In place of Styrofoam you can roll newspaper into a ball for the head and use two cone-shaped paper cups for the body. Stack the cups one inside the other so they are strong enough to support the head. Or you can make a tracing-paper pattern of the cone shape. You will need a piece of cardboard 9 inches by 5 inches. Trace the cone shape onto cardboard and cut it out. Roll it into a cone, overlap the edges slightly, and tape it. You will also need newspaper, water, wallpaper paste or flour, and a bowl for papier-mâché.

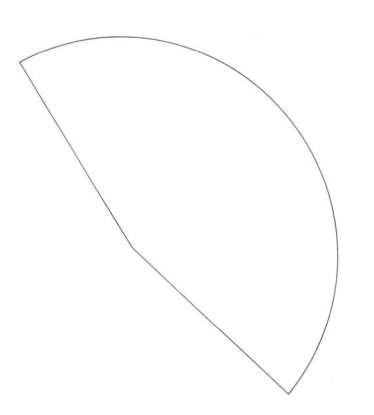

Full-size pattern on page 99

1. Tape the ball to the top of the cone.

2. Prepare the wallpaper paste mixture (see page 8) and cover the entire ball and cone with one layer of papier-mâché.

3. Wait at least 24 hours, and when the papier-mâché is totally dry, paint the doll a solid, light color. Then use the pencil to draw in the Czechoslovakian maid's features and costume. Give her a cap, a vest, and an apron, and don't forget to draw in her arms along the sides of her body. Use bright colors to paint the costume and details, and for extra emphasis outline her costume with a thin black line.

RAG DOLL

*Courtesy Brooklyn
Children's Museum*

18

Rag dolls have been made for thousands of years, since ancient Rome and probably before, and they are still being made all over the world today. They come in different shapes and sizes, but they all are made from scraps of fabric and leftover odds and ends.

There is usually extra fabric around every household, whether it is left over from another sewing project or a piece of a worn-out pair of trousers or a dress. The only tools you need to make a rag doll are a scissors and a needle and thread.

A simple rag doll was made famous in the early 1900's by artist Johnny Gruelle. He found an old soft cloth doll tucked away in his mother's attic; he gave the doll to his daughter, who fell in love with her. He created a book about the doll, and named her Raggedy Ann.

The rag doll pictured here, like Raggedy Ann, was made in the United States around the turn of the century. She was made from a pattern that people bought at their local sewing or yard-goods stores. Her body is a simple outline shape, and the front is the same as the back. She's called a rag doll, but she's so fresh and pretty that you wouldn't know she's made from leftovers.

General Supplies:

A pencil, white chalk, a ruler, scissors, tracing paper (one piece must be 18 inches long and 10 inches wide—tape two smaller pieces together if you don't have paper this size), straight pins, masking tape, a needle and thread, and newspapers.

You will need a piece of white fabric 18 by 24 inches to make the doll. Use felt, cotton, or muslin. If you use cotton or muslin you will need an iron, so you can iron down the ragged edges of the fabric before you sew the doll together. You will need scraps of fabric to stuff the doll, and inks, tempera paint, felt-tipped markers, or crayons to draw or paint the face and hair. For the dress use a pretty fabric 24 by 14 inches, and for the collar a piece of white felt 8 inches square. You will need 3 pieces of ribbon, each 12 inches long; another piece of felt approximately 8 inches square for the shoes; and eight pieces of colored tissue or crepe paper, each 4 by 4 inches, for the flowers.

1. Make a tracing-paper pattern of the doll (see page 10). Because the doll is too large for one page of this book the pattern has been broken up into two parts, A and B. To transfer it in one piece onto the tracing paper, fold the tracing paper in half lengthwise to make a rectangle 18 inches long and 5 inches wide. With the fold on the left, place the top of the tracing paper over part A; the pattern tells you which edge to line up with the fold in the tracing paper. Trace around the top half of the doll, including the broken line. Then place the tracing paper over part B. The pattern tells you which edge to line up

Full-size patterns on pages 100, 101

20

with the fold in the tracing paper, and the broken line on the tracing paper should be placed directly on top of the broken line in part B. Continue to trace around the bottom half of the doll. Cut out the pattern, through both layers of tracing paper, and open it up.

2. You now have a full-size doll pattern. Trace the pattern onto the white fabric twice—once for the back of the doll, once for the front. *Do not cut them out.*

3. If your material is thin enough for paint to soak through, put down several layers of newspaper to protect your work surface, and lay the fabric flat. Paint the rag doll's face and hair on one piece, and the back of her hair on the other.

4. Now cut out each piece. If you used cotton or muslin, the edges will be ragged, so lay out each of the pieces with the painted side facing down. Turn in an 1/8-inch border and iron it down. (You may want to have an adult help you with this.)

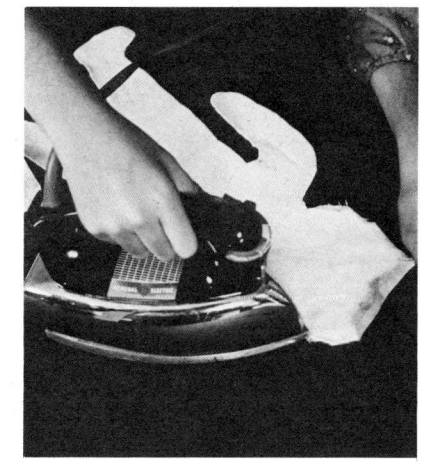

5. Lay out the back piece with the painted side facing down. Place the front piece, with the painted face showing, directly on top of the back piece. Line up the edges of the back and front, and begin to sew the doll together.

6. Use an overcast stitch (see page 4) to sew the front and the back together around the head, then stuff the head with scraps of fabric. Sew the arms together and stuff them. Then sew the rag doll along her sides and around her legs leaving the feet open. Stuff the rest of her body and legs, and then sew the feet closed.

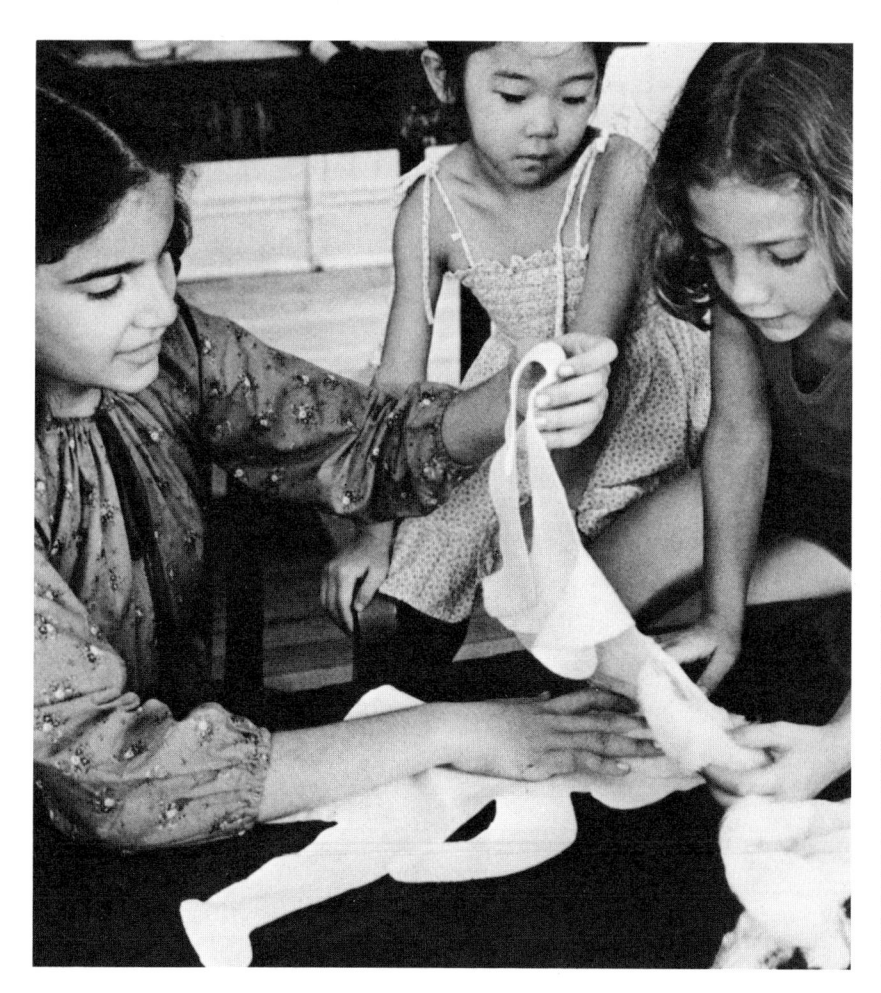

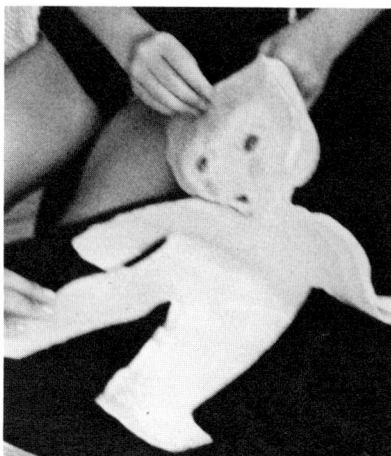

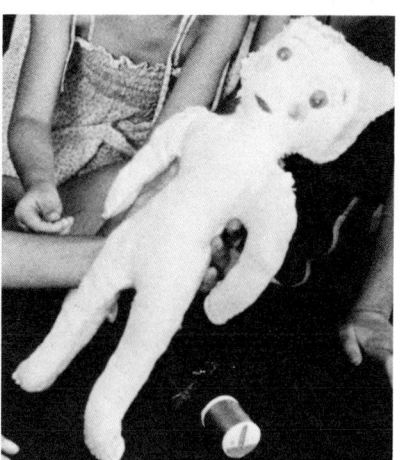

Full-size pattern on page 102

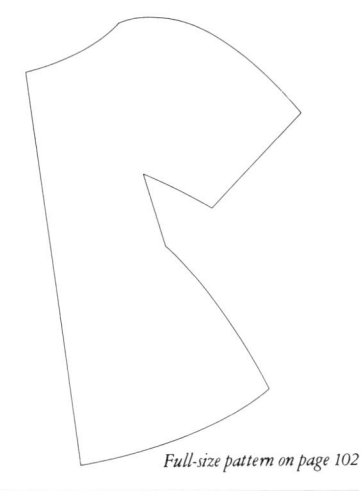

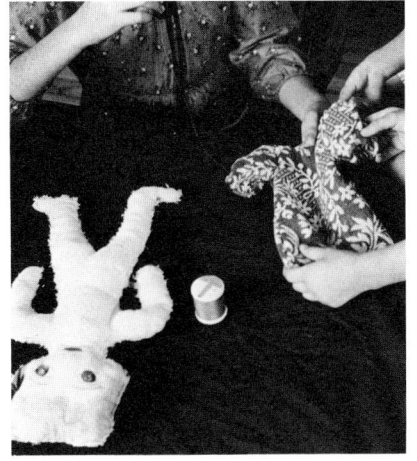

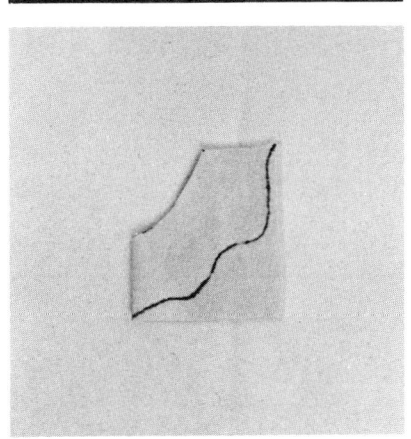

7. To make the dress: Fold the dress fabric into quarters (see page 6) to make a rectangle 12 inches long and 7 inches wide. Make a tracing-paper pattern of the dress (see page 10). Line up the straight, left side of the pattern against the second fold in the fabric, as the pattern indicates. Trace around the pattern and cut out the dress, through all four layers of fabric. You will have two pieces, one for the back, the other for the front of the dress. Lay one piece directly on top of the other and stitch the two pieces together along the shoulders, the sleeves, and the sides. Leave the neckline, the openings for the arms, and the hem of the dress unsewn.

8. Put the dress on over the doll's head. Gather the ends of the sleeves around each arm with a running stitch (see page 5).

9. To cover the stitches, tie a piece of ribbon in a bow around the end of each sleeve.

10. To make the collar: Fold the 8-inch square of felt into quarters, to make a 4-inch square. Measure and cut a 2-inch neckline (see page 7). Leave the felt folded and draw a wavy line connecting the lower left and upper right corners. Cut along this wavy line, through all four layers of felt. Make the collar lacey by cutting a "snowflake" pattern: Leaving the felt folded, cut triangles, squares, squiggles—any kind of small shapes—along the folded edges.

11. Open up the collar and put it over the rag doll's head. Use a running stitch to gather the collar around her neck.

12. Tie a bow with the third piece of ribbon, and stitch it to the side of the rag doll's painted hair.

13. To make the shoes: Make a tracing-paper pattern and trace 4 shoe shapes onto the felt. Cut them out. Place one directly on top of another and sew the two pieces together; stitch around the entire shape except for the curved top edge. Repeat this and sew the other two shoe shapes together.

14. Put one shoe on each foot. To hold them in place sew the shoes onto the doll's feet with a stitch or two at each heel.

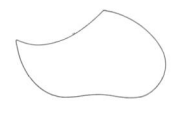

Full-size pattern on page 102

15. To make the flowers that decorate the shoes (make each flower separately): Take four of the pieces of tissue or crepe paper and place them one on top of the other. You will be folding them together into a strip with accordion pleats. Begin working from the side nearest you and fold the end up ¼ inch.

16. Turn the stack over, so the fold is still at the end nearest you and the folded ¼-inch strip is flat against your work surface. Again, fold the 4-inch side nearest you up ¼ inch.

17. Turn the stack over again. Repeat steps 15 and 16 until the tissue paper is all folded into one ¼-inch-wide strip.

18. Fold the strip in half from left to right. Wrap a piece of tape around the fold to hold the paper together.

19. Separate and spread out the layers of tissue paper. Make a second flower with the remaining four pieces of tissue paper.

20. Stitch one flower to the front of each shoe.

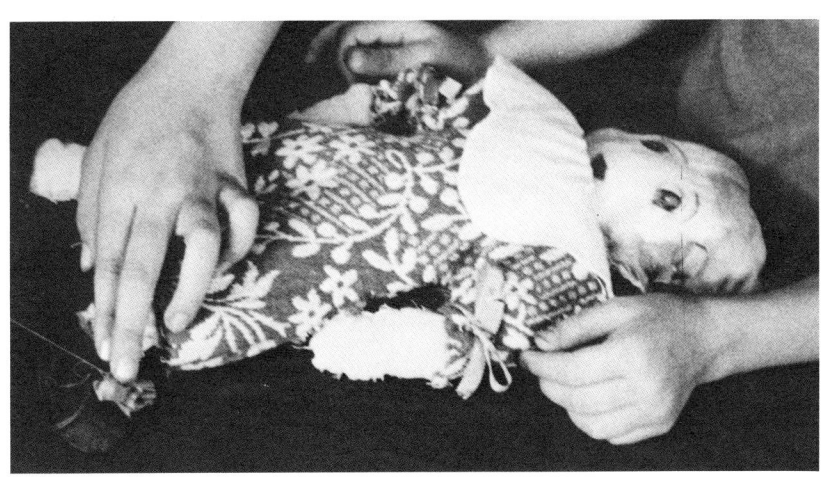

RAG BROOM DOLL

*Courtesy Brooklyn
Children's Museum*

This rag doll isn't so cuddly, because she is made out of a hard leftover household item—an old broom. In Colonial days people made their own brooms. When one wore out, a thrifty mother or older sister would often turn a small broom into a doll for a younger child to play with.

This doll was made in America about one hundred years ago, and is called a rag doll because she was dressed in leftover squares of fabric that were simply folded and tied around her body.

General Supplies:

White chalk, scissors, a needle, and thread.

You will need a small whisk broom about 9 inches high (if you don't have one around your house, you can buy one at most hardware or household goods stores), a black sock for the doll's head, and scraps of fabric to stuff it. You will need a piece of plain fabric 12 inches long and 18 inches wide for the dress, and a strip of ¼-inch-wide ribbon 18 inches long to tie around the broom doll's neck. A 14-inch square of fabric will be needed for the shawl, and an 8-inch square for the turban wrapped around her head. Use gingham, calico, or any brightly colored fabrics for these.

1. To make the broom doll's head, stuff the toe of the sock with scraps of fabric.

2. Hold the broom so the narrow end is on top and the wide whisk part is on the bottom. Put the sock over the broom. The stuffed toe will sit on top of the broom and form the doll's head.

3. To make the dress: Lay out the piece of 12-by-18-inch fabric. Use a running stitch to gather the fabric (see page 5) along one of the 18-inch sides. Wrap the dress around the broom, with the gathered edge under the neck, and stitch it closed at the neck.

4. To cover the stitches and secure the head, tie the ribbon in a bow around the doll's neck.

5. To make the cape: Fold the 14-inch square of fabric in half diagonally. Drape the folded fabric around the doll's shoulders and sew the front together with one or two stitches to keep it in place.

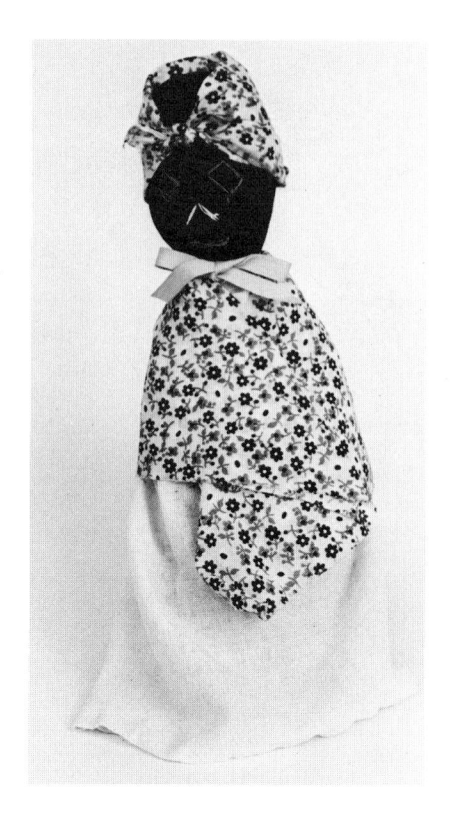

6. To make the doll's face, use white chalk and draw diamonds for eyes, an upside-down V for a nose, and a straight or curved line for the mouth. Stitch over these lines with a needle and colored thread.

7. To make the turban: Fold the 8-inch square of fabric in half diagonally. With the folded edge along the top, wrap the fabric around the back of the doll's head and tie the ends in a knot at the front.

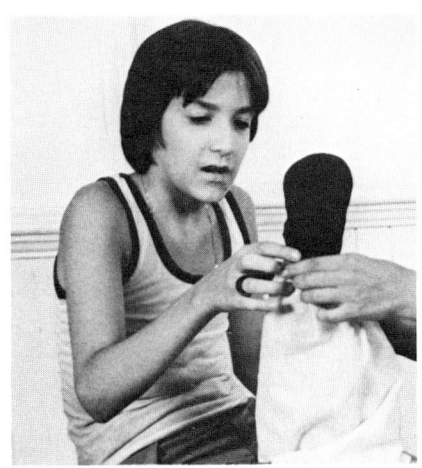

COLIMA CLAY DOLL

© Justin Kerr, 1981

You need special tools to make something out of hard materials like wood or stone, but clay is soft and easy to work with. Clay is found in most parts of the world, and people of many cultures have used it to make dolls.

Flat terra-cotta clay dolls have been discovered in a part of Western Mexico called Colima. The dolls were made from a dark-red clay, and by testing the clay we can say that they are over a thousand years old. But we are not sure what the dolls were used for. They look like flat cookies or gingerbread men. Some may be musicians and some seem to be playing ball. Some are just people carrying baskets, or babies sleeping in clay cradles.

There are many different types of clay. The most commonly available for crafts is plasticine, or modeling clay, which never hardens. It is soft, easy to work with, and dries when exposed to the air. There is a product called Miracle Clay, sold in many art stores, which is also soft; but you can bake Miracle Clay in your kitchen oven to make it hard, and the doll you make out of it will be more permanent than one made out of plasticine. There is Play-Doh, and a wide variety of other brightly colored brand-name clays—ask about them at your local art or craft supply stores. In addition to clay you will need newspapers, a pencil, and a butter knife.

Working with clay is a matter of feel. The warmth from your hands will make the clay workable. You will make two basic shapes with the clay: a ball, made by rolling a chunk of clay between your two palms, and a snake, which you make by rolling a chunk of clay into a long rounded strip on a table. Fool around with the clay and the shapes to get the right proportions—it is easy to add or subtract some clay to make any part of the doll larger or smaller.

1. Spread the newspapers over your work surface. Roll a ball about the size of a half dollar for the doll's head. Put the ball on the newspaper and use your palm to flatten it out, making a circle about ¼ inch thick.

2. Take a larger chunk of clay and roll a ball about twice as big as the head for the body. Flatten the body with the palm of your hand. Overlap it slightly onto the head, so the two pieces attach. If the proportions don't seem exactly right, you can use the knife to cut from either the head or the body—or you can add a little clay to either.

3. To make the arms, roll two 3-inch-long snakes. Place one on each side of the body, overlapped slightly onto the body. Flatten each snake with your palm.

4. To make the legs, roll two 3-inch-long snakes. Place them at the bottom of the body, overlapped slightly onto it, and again flatten each with your palm.

5. Use your thumb to smooth out the parts of the doll and make sure they are well connected. You may need to add extra clumps of clay at the points where the head, legs, and arms connect with the body, to reinforce them.

6. To decorate the doll, roll tiny balls for the eyes and nose and a small snake for the mouth, and press them onto the doll's face. Or use the pencil to draw or engrave the doll's features. Draw a costume on the doll, or make it out of clay. You can roll a snake for a belt, or make shoes or a hat. Roll tiny balls and press them onto the doll for polka dots, or roll thin snakes for stripes.

7. Gently pick up the doll and lay it out on a fresh piece of newspaper. All clay hardens a bit when exposed to air. If you are using Miracle Clay, bake the doll, following the instructions on the package.

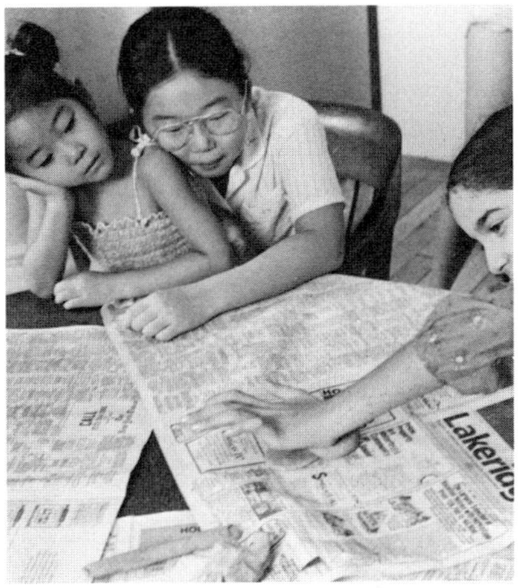
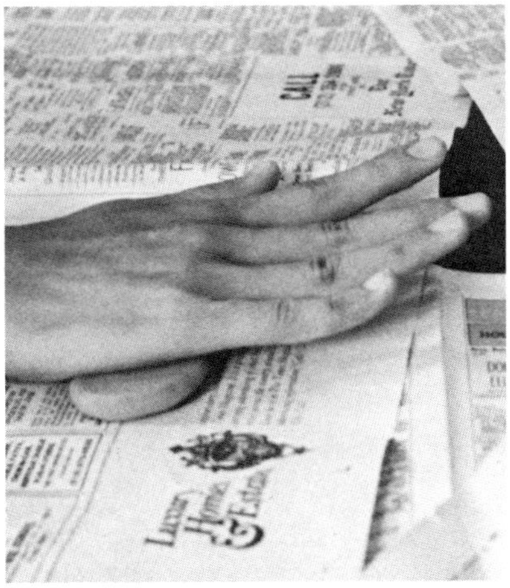
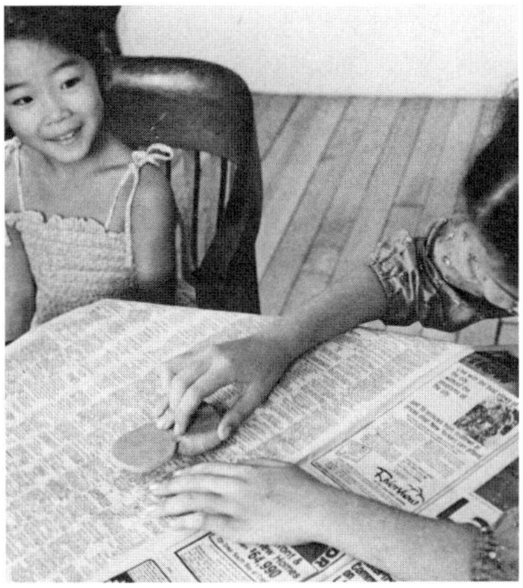
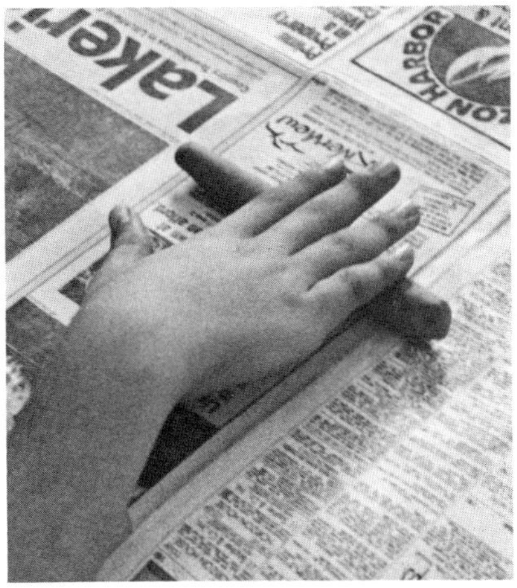
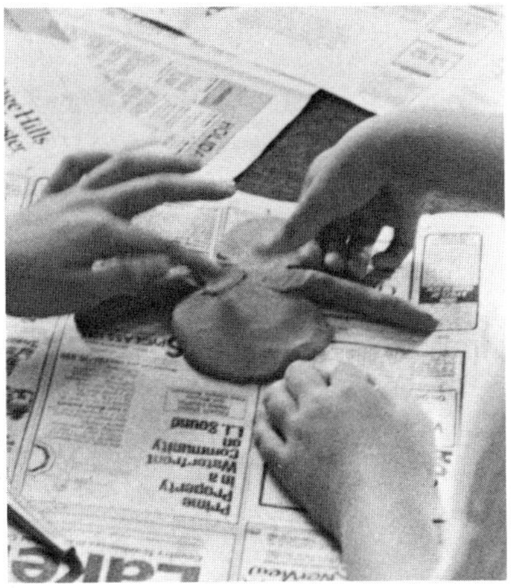
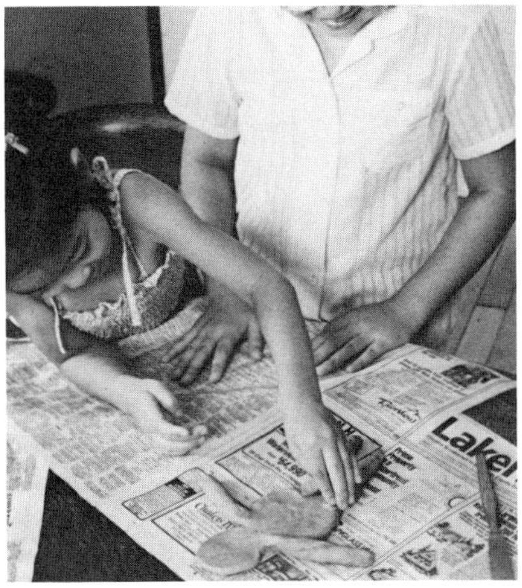
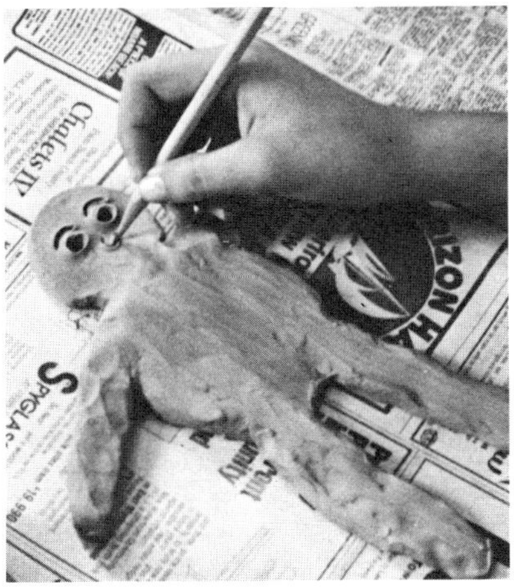
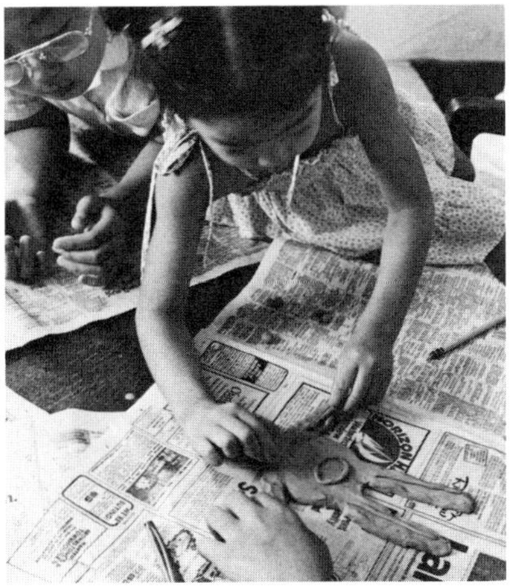
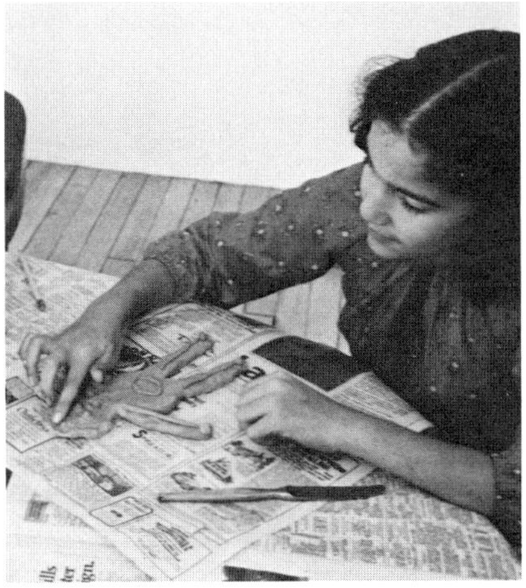

TURKISH SOCK DOLL

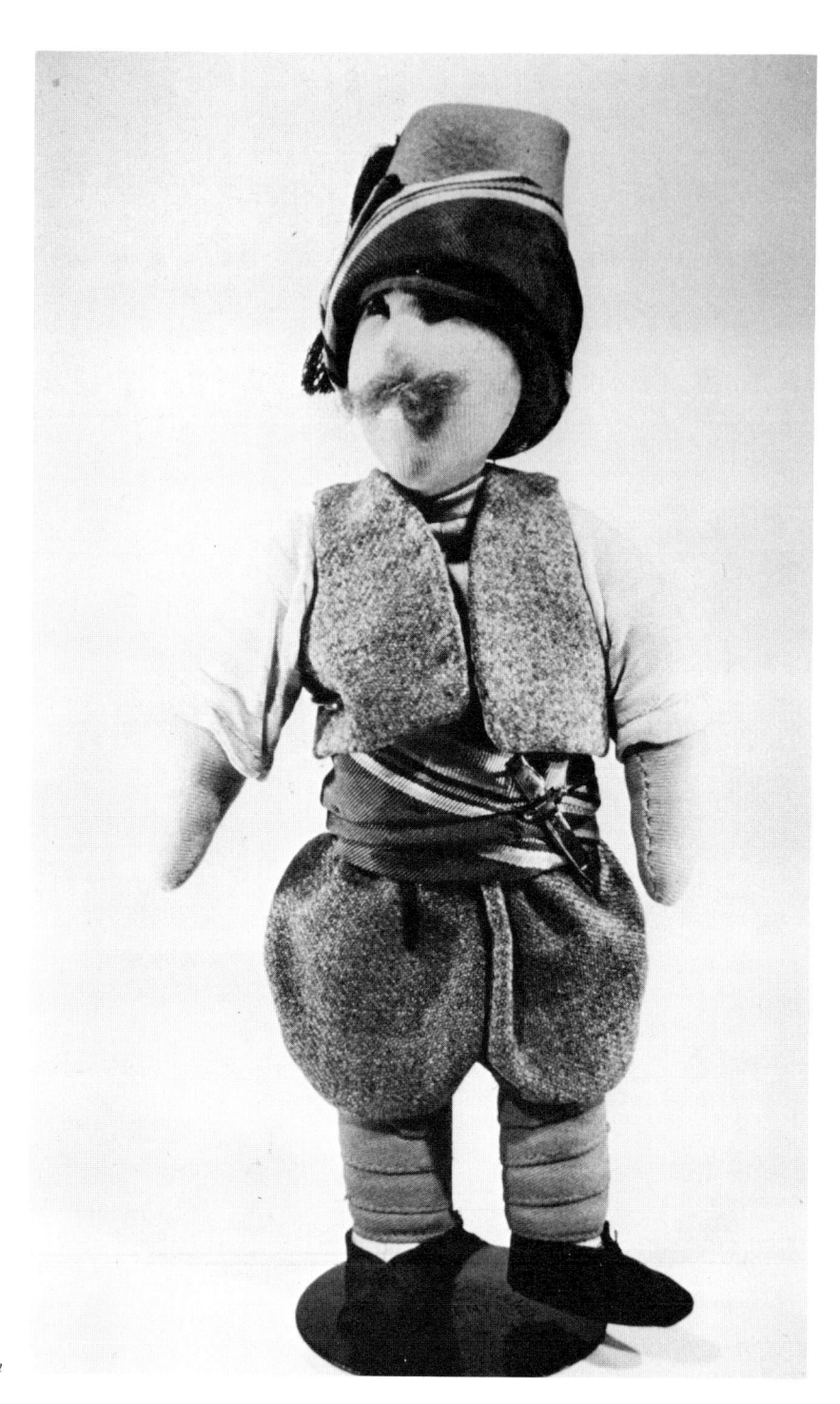

*Courtesy Brooklyn
Children's Museum*

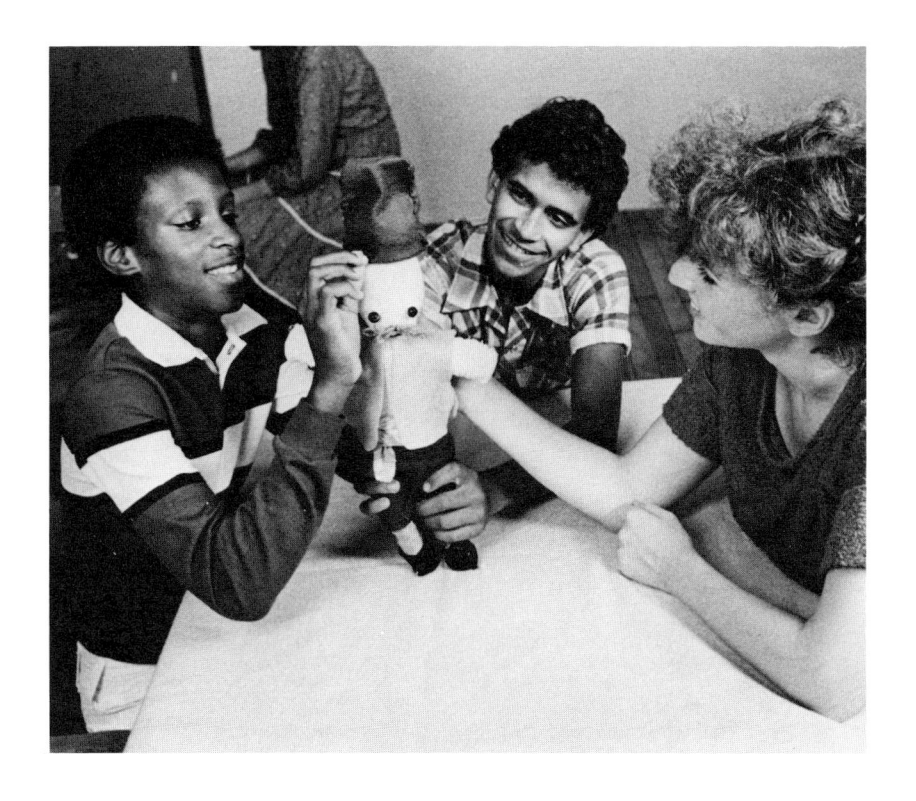

The first sock doll was probably made in the Middle Ages, because that's when people began wearing stockings. Just as we know early American mothers fashioned worn-out brooms into dolls, and for centuries people used leftover cloth to make rag dolls, it's easy to imagine a medieval mother, who was about to throw away an old stocking beyond mending, pausing and thinking about what a good doll it would make.

This doll from Turkey is made from a sock, and he wears a native costume: a vest, short pants, a sash, and a fez—a cap with a tassel, worn in many Mediterranean countries.

General Supplies:

A pencil, white chalk, a ruler, scissors, tracing paper, masking tape, straight pins, a needle, and thread.

You will need a knee sock, or any sock about 18 inches long, and scraps of fabric to stuff it. You will need two buttons for the doll's eyes; yarn for his neck, mustache, and tassel; and pieces of felt for the costume: 6 by 14 inches for the pants, 11 by 6½ inches for the vest, 6 inches square for the shoes, and 6 by 10 inches for the fez. Use a different color of felt for each article of clothing. You will also need two pieces of ¼-inch-wide ribbon, each 36 inches long, to wrap the doll's legs, and a piece of decorated fabric 10 inches square for the sash.

1. Lay out the sock vertically, flat against your work surface, so the toe is at the top. The toe of the sock will be the top of the doll's head, the open-ended cuff the bottom of the doll.

2. You will need two 2-inch strips cut from the cuff to make the doll's arms. Place the ruler with the zero at the cuff and measure and mark off 2 inches and 4 inches along both sides of the sock.

3. Draw a straight line connecting both 2-inch points and another straight line connecting both 4-inch points. Cut along each of these two straight lines, cutting through both the front and back of the sock.

4. Sew one of the strips closed along one long side. Stuff the strip with scraps and sew the other side closed. Repeat with the other strip. Put the arms aside while you work on the legs, head, and body.

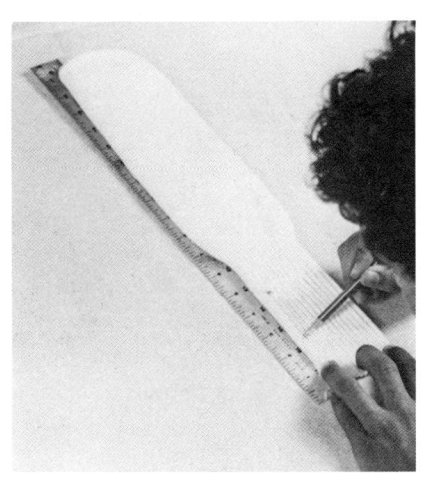

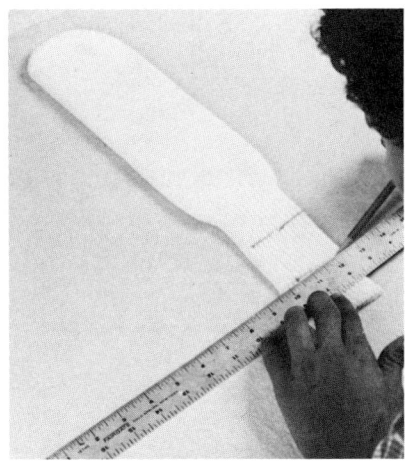

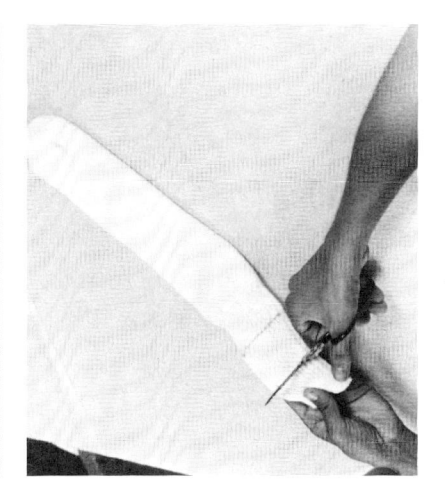

5. To make the legs, make a vertical line about 6 inches long up the center of the sock from the cuff toward the toe (head). Hold the front and back together and cut along this line, through both layers.

6. Stuff the top half of the doll with scraps.

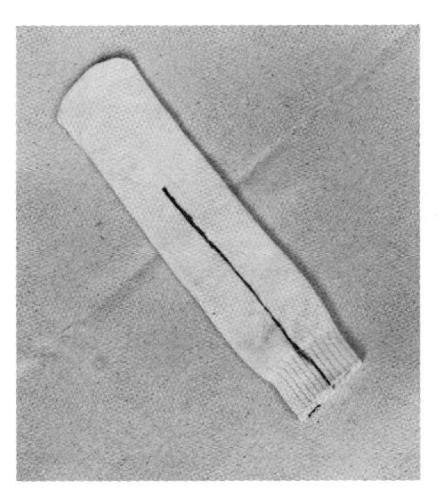

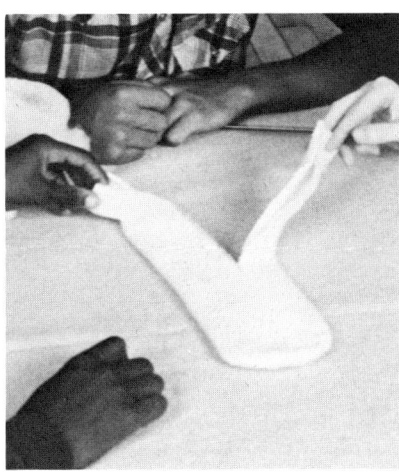

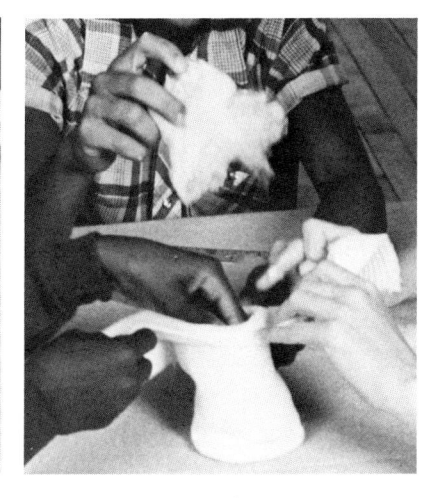

7. To form the head, measure 4 inches down from the toe toward the legs. Tie a piece of yarn around the doll at this point to make the neck.

8. Starting from the top of one leg, sew the side halfway closed and stuff it with scraps. Finish sewing the side of the leg and stuff the bottom portion. Repeat for the other leg. Sew the bottoms of the legs closed.

9. Sew one arm to each side of the body just under the neck.

10. Sew on the button eyes.

11. To make the doll's mustache, cut five 3-inch-long pieces of yarn. Line them up evenly and gather them together. Cut another piece of yarn 6 inches long, and tie it around the middle of the bunch. Sew the mustache on the doll.

12. To wrap the legs, sew the end of one piece of ribbon around the bottom of either leg. Starting at the bottom, wrap the ribbon around and up the leg in a spiral. When you get to the end of the ribbon, sew it to the leg at that point. Repeat this for the other leg.

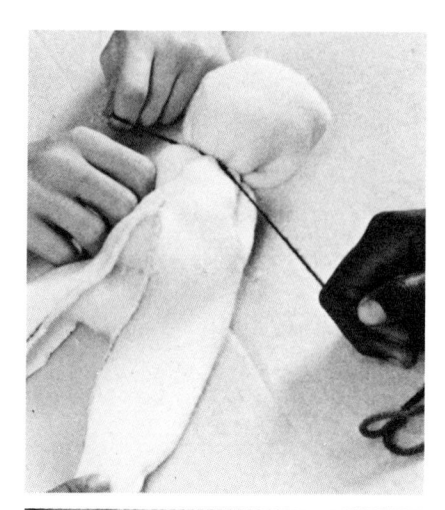

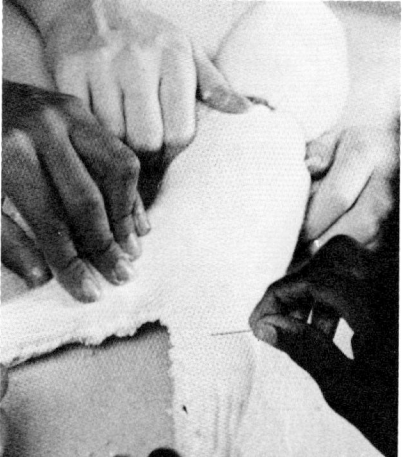

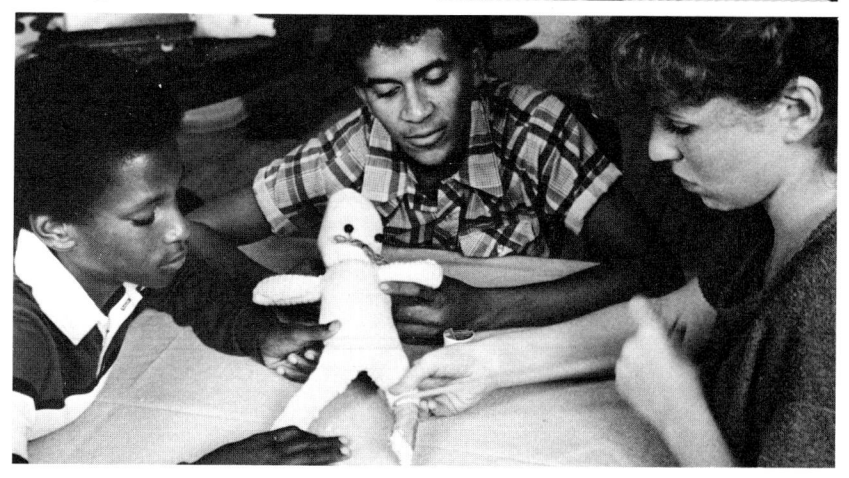

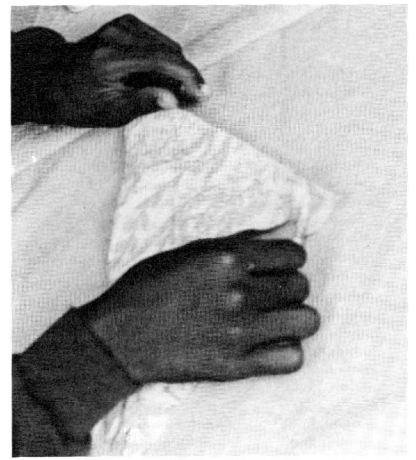

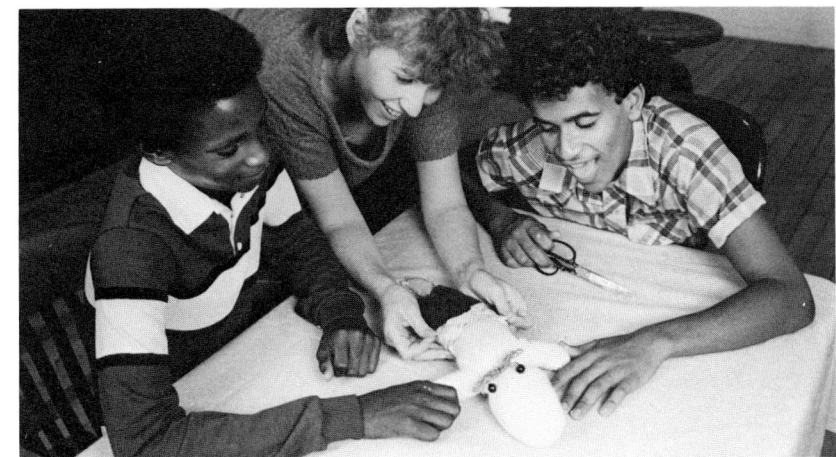

Full-size patterns on pages 103, 104

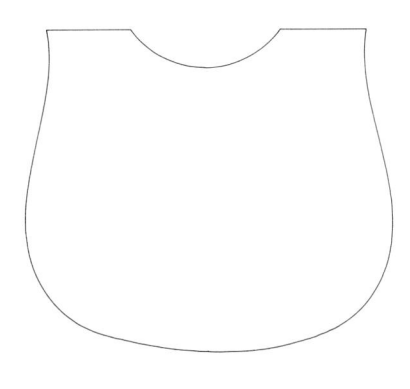

13. To make the pants: Make a tracing-paper pattern (see page 10). Trace two patterns onto the 6-by-14-inch felt (one for the front, the other for the back of the pants). Cut out the two pieces. Place one directly on top of the other, line up the edges, and sew them together along the inner and outer pant legs. Do not sew across the waist or the cuffs.

14. Put the pants on the doll. Use a running stitch (see page 5) to gather the cuffs of the pants around the doll's legs.

15. To make the sash: Fold the 10-inch square of fabric in half diagonally. Tie the sash around the doll's waist, with a knot at the side.

16. To make the vest: Fold the 11-by-6½-inch fabric in half from top to bottom to make a rectangle 5½ inches long and 6½ inches wide. Make a tracing-paper pattern, line up the fold of the fabric with the pattern according to the instructions on the pattern, and pin the pattern to the fabric. Trace around the pattern and cut out the vest through both layers of fabric.

17. Put the vest on over the doll's head. Stitch the front and the back of the vest together down each side under the doll's arms. Cut the front of the vest open down the middle.

18. To make the shoes: Make a tracing-paper pattern and trace four shoe shapes onto the felt. Cut them out. Place one directly on top of another and sew the two pieces together. Stitch around the entire shape except for the straight top edge. Repeat this with the two remaining shoe shapes. Put the shoes on the doll's feet and sew a stitch or two at each heel to hold it in place.

19. To make the fez: Make a tracing-paper pattern of the fez. Trace two patterns onto the 6-by-10-inch felt, one for the front, the other for the back. Cut them out. Place one piece directly on top of the other, line up the edges, and sew them together along the top and each side; do not sew along the bottom. This will be the brim. Turn the bottom up about 1 inch to make the brim, and put the fez on the doll's head. Cock, or tip, the hat so it sits on his head at a slight angle.

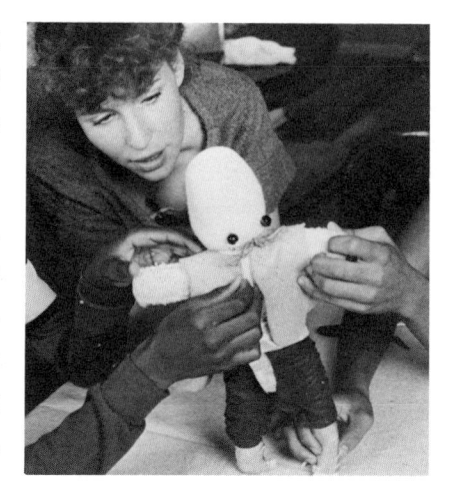

Full-size patterns on page 105

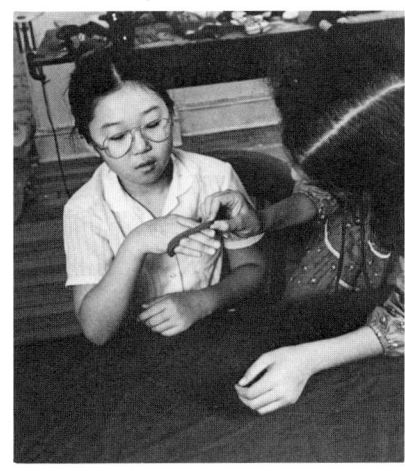

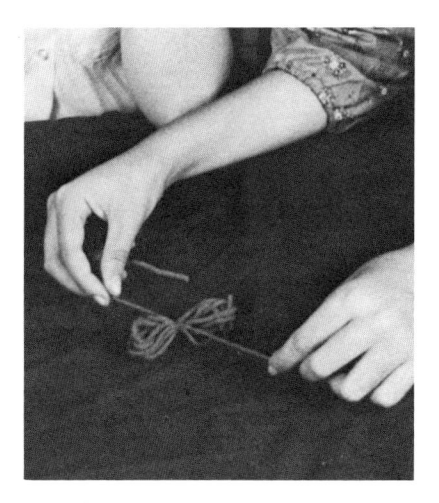

20. To make the tassel for the fez: Wrap yarn around your four outstretched fingers about a dozen times.

21. Slide the loops of wrapped yarn off your hand.

22. Pinch the loops together in the center. Use a piece of yarn 12 inches long to tie them around the middle. Cut through the looped ends of the wrapped yarn, but do not cut off the ends of the 12-inch piece, which will remain longer than the rest.

23. To attach the tassel to the fez, sew the ends of the 12-inch piece of yarn to the top corner of the hat at one side.

INDIAN CORNHUSK DOLLS

*Photographs courtesy
Museum of the American Indian,
Heye Foundation*

Corn was so plentiful in America that Indians used it for many different things. No part of the corn was wasted. They roasted ears of corn over roaring fires, cooked it up into pots of succotash (a corn-and-lima-bean stew), and ground it up, added water, and baked thin, tortillalike breads. They also softened the brittle outer husks of the corn in water and wove them into mats to sleep on and baskets to store and carry food—and they used them to make cornhusk dolls. Some of the dolls were used for special feasts and ceremonies. Others were playthings that young Indian girls strapped to their backs like papooses, just as modern children lay dolls into doll carriages to imitate the way parents care for children.

The settlers made cornhusk dolls too—the Indians taught them how to make them.

Iroquois Cornhusk Doll
(shown on page 42, left)

This cornhusk doll was made by the Iroquois Indians of upstate New York, and is dressed in a typical Iroquois costume, with a fringed buckskin shirt and feather headband.

General Supplies:

A pencil, white chalk, a ruler, scissors, tracing paper, masking tape, straight pins, white glue, a needle, and thread.

You will need about a dozen dried cornhusks. You can buy bags of cornhusks at most craft supply stores, and because they are used in Mexican cooking, you can also buy them in many Mexican and gourmet food stores. Or you can dry your own husks: Strip the husks off ears of fresh corn. Remove the silk and spread the husks on newspapers for a few days to dry. (In place of cornhusks you can use strips of crepe paper 1 inch wide and 7 inches long.) You will need a bowl and water to soak the husks, a towel, and thread to tie the husks together. To make the body sturdier, you will make a frame out of wire. You will need three pieces of medium-weight wire, two 12 inches long and one 6 inches long, to make the frame.

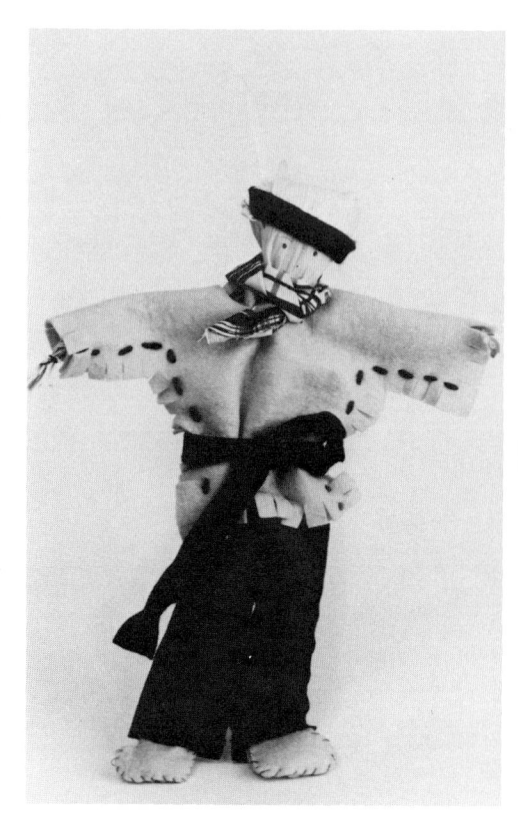

Make the costume out of felt—it will be easy to cut fringes on the shirt, and felt has the soft look of buckskin, which is what the Indians actually used. For the pants you will need a piece of felt 6 inches long and 9 inches wide; for the shirt a piece 12 inches long and 10 inches wide; and for the moccasins, a piece approximately 5 inches square. For the belt, use a strip of felt or ribbon ½ inch wide by 18 inches long, and for the headband a piece of ribbon or felt 8 inches long by ½ inch wide. For the scarf, use a 6-inch-square piece of decorated fabric. For extra color, sew the shirt and the pants with colored yarn instead of thread. You will also need a black felt-tipped marker and two feathers. You can buy feathers at a craft store, get them from a pet shop, or make them out of construction paper.

1. Soak the cornhusks in a bowl of water for about 20 minutes. Shake off the excess water and lay them out on the towel so they retain some of their moisture while you're working with them. (If you are using crepe paper, skip this step.)

2. To make the doll's head, hold one piece of 12-inch wire upright. Bend a cornhusk over the top of the wire. Gather the open ends of the husk around the wire and wrap a piece of thread around them. Tie the ends of the thread together. This will form the doll's neck. Repeat this, using one or two more husks, until the head is rounded and smooth.

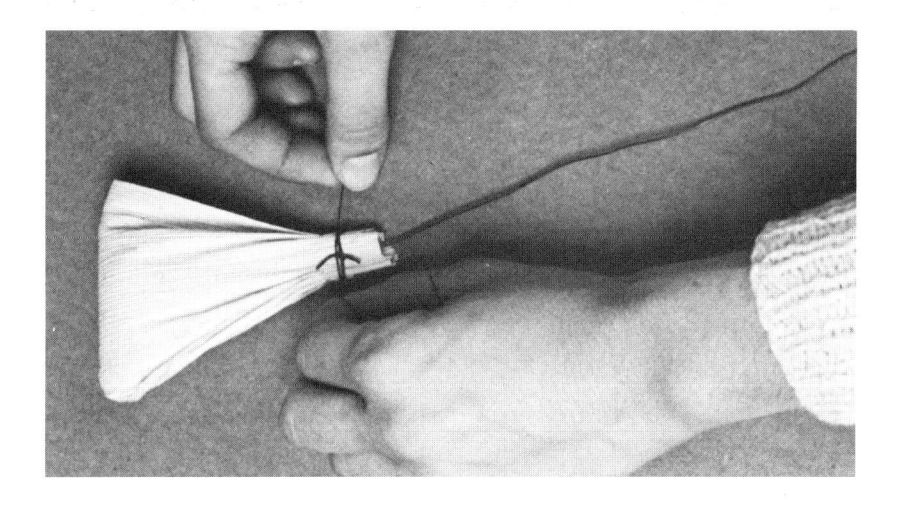

3. To make the arms, lay out the other 12-inch piece of wire. It will take two husks to cover it. Start at one end and wrap a husk around the wire. Use thread to tie both ends of the husk in place. Wrap the second husk around the other end of the wire and tie it in place. The second husk will overlap the first around the middle.

4. To attach the arms, hold the first piece of wire upright. Hold the arms horizontally across the front of this piece, just under the doll's neck. Wrap a long piece of thread around the two pieces several times in a criss-cross fashion. Tie the ends of the thread together.

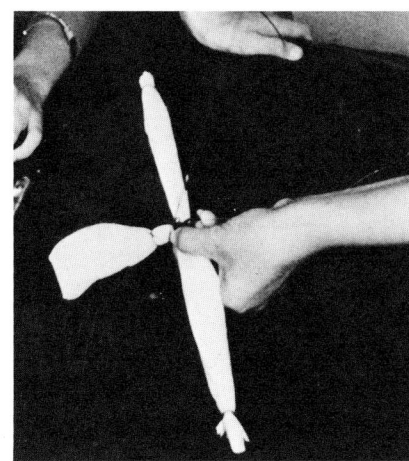

5. To cover the body, wrap cornhusks around the rest of the wire and tie them in place, as you did with the arms.

6. The bottom half of the body forms one of the doll's legs. To make the other leg, wrap one cornhusk around the 6-inch piece of wire and tie it into place at both ends of the wire. (If the husk is longer than the wire, cut off the excess husk.)

7. To attach the second leg, lay the body flat and place the leg on top of the body. Line up the bottom of the second leg with the bottom of the body. Use thread to tie the top of the second leg in place around the doll's waist. This leg will slide over to one side slightly when you tie it on.

8. Wait until the cornhusks are completely dry and draw in the doll's face with the felt-tipped marker.

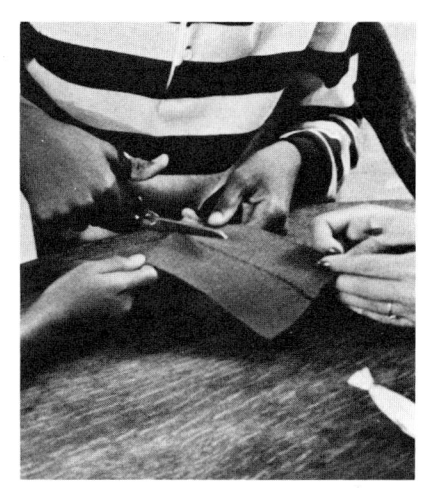

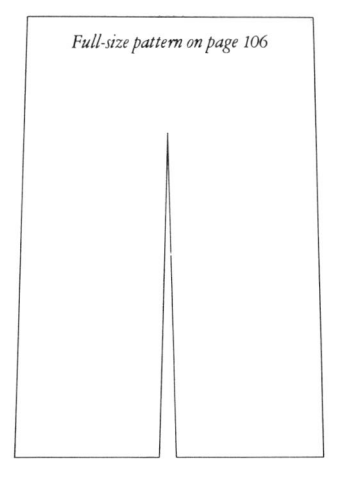

Full-size pattern on page 106

9. To make the pants: Make a tracing-paper pattern of the pants (see page 10). Trace two patterns onto the 6-by-9-inch felt, one for the back, the other for the front of the pants, and cut them out. Place one piece directly on top of the other, line up the edges, and sew them together along the inner and outer pant legs. Do not sew across the waist or the cuffs.

10. To make the shirt: Fold the 12-by-10-inch felt into quarters (see page 6) to make a rectangle 6 inches long and 5 inches wide. Make a tracing-paper pattern, line up the fold of the fabric with the pattern according to the instructions on the pattern, and pin the pattern to the felt. Trace around the pattern and cut out the shirt, through all four layers of felt.

11. Open up the shirt from right to left, leaving it folded from top to bottom. To make the fringe, make ¼-inch cuts ½ inch apart along the sides, the insides of the sleeves, the cuffs, and the bottom edge of the shirt. You will sew the shirt together when you put it on the doll.

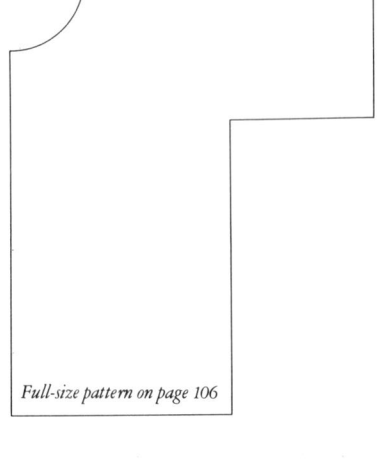

Full-size pattern on page 106

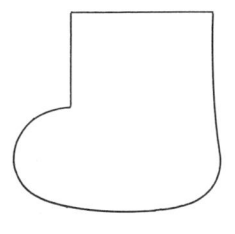

Full-size pattern on page 106

12. To make the moccasins: Make a tracing-paper pattern and trace four moccasin shapes onto the felt. Cut them out. Place one directly on top of another and stitch the two pieces together around the entire shape, except for the straight, top edge. Repeat this with the other two moccasin shapes.

13. Dress the doll. Put on the pants. Put the shirt on over the doll's head, line up the edges, and sew it together inside the fringe along the sleeves and down the sides. Tie the belt around the waist. Put the moccasins on the doll's feet.

14. Fold the 6-inch square of fabric in half diagonally. Tie it in a knot around the doll's neck.

15. Wrap the headband around the top of the doll's head. The ends of the strip will overlap slightly. Sew a stitch or two to hold the headband in place, and glue feathers inside the back of the headband.

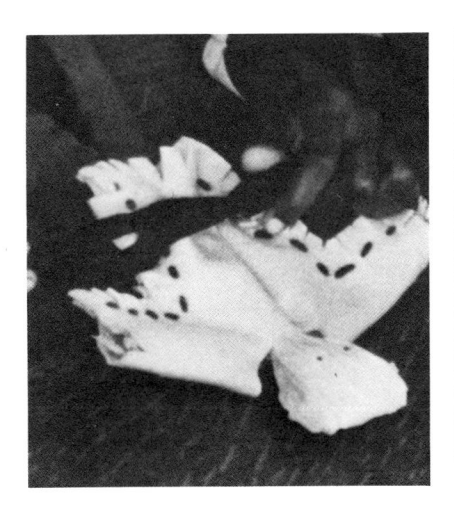

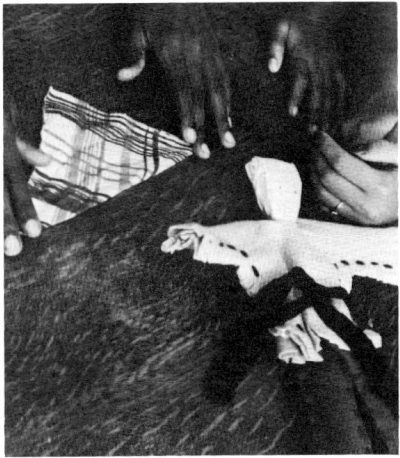

Odas
(shown on page 42, right)

The Delaware Indians made a sacred cornhusk doll called an Odas. It was believed that an Odas protected her owner's health, and it is likely that each family in the tribe had its own doll. Every spring, to honor the season of planting and renewal, this husk doll was given a dance and new clothes. The owner called an Odas his or her "grandmother."

General Supplies:

A pencil or white chalk, a ruler, scissors, a needle, and thread.

You will need about fourteen dried cornhusks. (See page 44 for information on drying your own or buying bags of cornhusks, or substituting crepe paper.) You will also need water, a bowl, a towel, and thread. You will need a piece of wire 12 inches long to make the frame of the doll.

As you see from the photograph, an Odas wears a fabulous outfit—a dress covered with silver ornaments, long streamers of fabric, and countless rows of beads. Use a 20-by-14-inch piece of fabric for the dress. You will need about two dozen strips of brightly colored fabric for the streamers. Use cotton, satin, or any lightweight material. The streamers should be varying lengths and widths, from about ¼ to 1½ inches wide, and about 8 to 14 inches long. For the ornaments use eyelets, which are sold at sewing stores; metal washers or nuts, which can be purchased at hardware stores; paper clips;

paper fasteners; circles made out of small pieces of wire; or a combination of these things. You can buy packages of beads at most five-and-tens, or at sewing or craft stores. To make a necklace for the doll, thread a needle, tie a knot at one end of the thread, and slip it through one bead at a time. When the necklace is the length you want, tie the ends of the thread together. String about a dozen rows, in varying colors and lengths, to drape around the Odas' neck. Also, collect some small bells or pieces from discarded costume jewelry to hang from the strings of beads, or use some of the leftover ornaments.

1. Soak the cornhusks in a bowl of water for about 20 minutes. Shake off the excess water and lay them out on the towel so they retain some of their moisture while you're working with them. (If you are using crepe paper, skip this step.)

2. To make the Odas' head, hold the 12-inch piece of wire upright. Bend a cornhusk over the top of the wire. Gather the open ends of the husk around the wire and wrap a piece of thread around them. Tie the ends of the thread together. This will form the doll's neck. Repeat this two or three more times until the head is rounded.

3. Cornhusks are wider at one end than the other. With the narrower end just under the neck, place four or five strips upright around the wire to make the doll's body. Hold them while you take a piece of thread and tie the tops of the husks in place. Do not tie them at the bottom.

4. Layer four or five more husks on top of the first group. Again, tie the tops and leave the bottoms of the cornhusks free.

5. Wait at least 24 hours, until the cornhusks are completely dry. Gather streamers of fabric around the doll's body, just under her neck. Tie them in place. Make a second layer and tie that in place. Use as many streamers as necessary to cover the cornhusks.

6. To make the Odas' dress: Fold the fabric into quarters (see page 6) to make a 10-by-7-inch rectangle. Measure and cut a ½-inch neckline (see page 7).

7. Open up the dress. Decorate it by sewing silvery ornaments all over the front and the back.

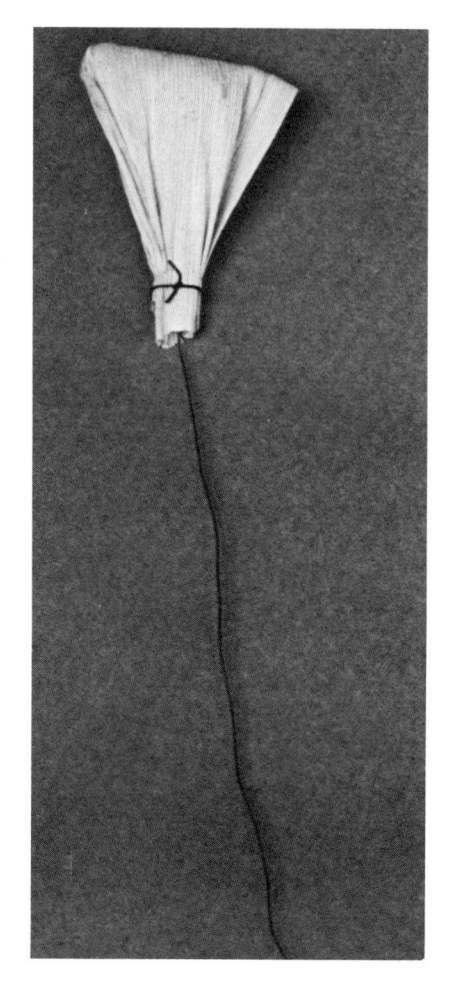

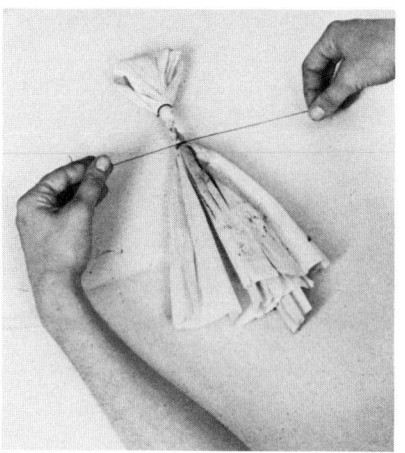

8. Put the dress on over the Odas' head. Use a running stitch (see page 5) to gather the neckline of the dress tightly around her neck.

9. String the beads around her neck and hang ornaments from the beads.

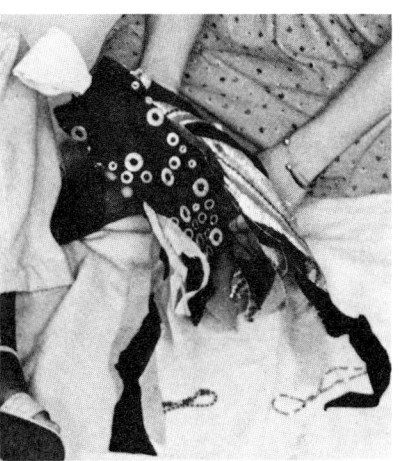

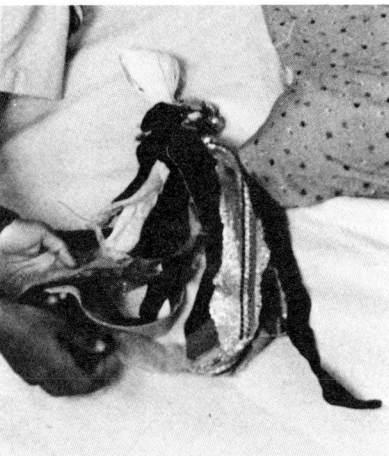

PANTIN

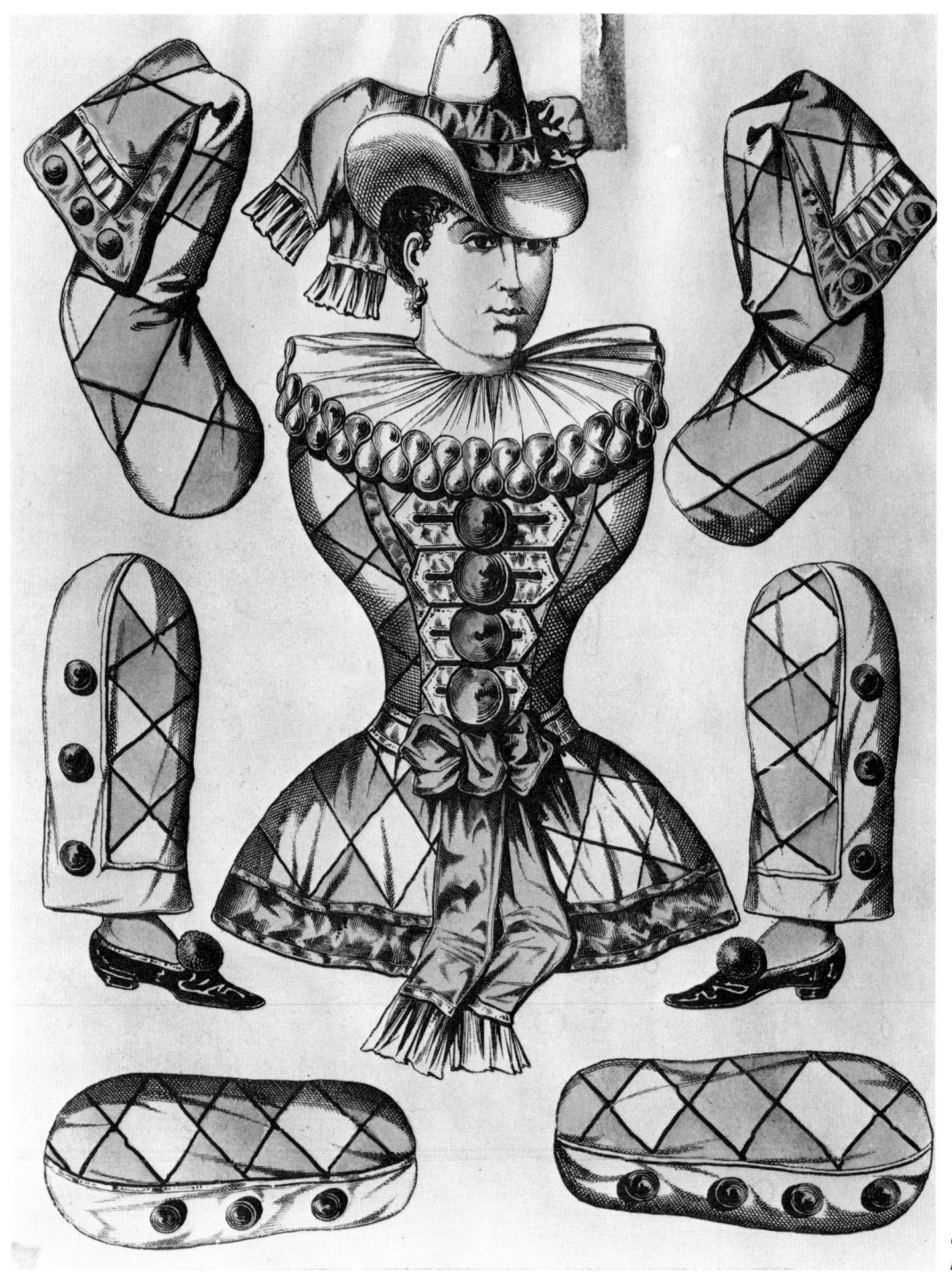

Courtesy Museum of the City of New York

Paper is another material which people all over the world use to make dolls. Doll makers of every culture have used their imaginations to make paper dolls that are more than flat, pretty cut-out pictures. The Japanese make origami dolls, with thickly folded paper costumes. In Europe and America paper dolls are given whole wardrobes of paper clothes. And in the eighteenth century, the French made a paper doll whose arms and legs were attached with strings at the doll's back. This doll was called a pantin—and if you pulled the pantin's strings, he jumped and danced.

The pantin was originally a children's toy, but it quickly became a fad among adults. While children had simple pantins, which they often made and decorated themselves, nobles commissioned famous artists at great expense to design pantins for them. Shepherds and kings, minstrels and judges, all kinds of characters were pantins. Adults soon lost interest in the pantins, but children continued to play with the dolls. And the word "pantin" eventually became part of the French vocabulary: Because the pantin doll jumps when someone pulls his strings, a person who is indecisive, or lets other people lead him around, is called a pantin. Today we have similar dolls called jumping jacks.

General Supplies:

A pencil, scissors, tracing paper, carbon paper, and crayons, colored pencils, or paints and a paintbrush.

You will need a piece of cardboard or oaktag 9 by 12 inches, and string. You will also need six paper fasteners to join the arms and legs to the body.

1. Make a tracing-paper pattern (see page 10) of all of the parts of the pantin. Trace them onto the oaktag or cardboard. Use carbon paper and trace the dots. Do not cut out the pieces.

2. Color in the pantin, then cut it out. Use the point of the scissors to make holes where the dots are.

3. With paper fasteners, attach the arms and legs behind the body.

4. Connect the arms across the back of the pantin by tying a string through each of the smaller holes above the paper fasteners.

5. Connect the legs across the back of the pantin in the same way.

6. Tie an 18-inch piece of string to the center of the string connecting the arms.

7. Let the string hang down, and tie it to the middle of the string connecting the legs. Let the extra string dangle down between the pantin's legs.

8. Tie a 4-inch piece of string to the pantin's head.

9. To make the pantin dance, hold the top string and pull the bottom string.

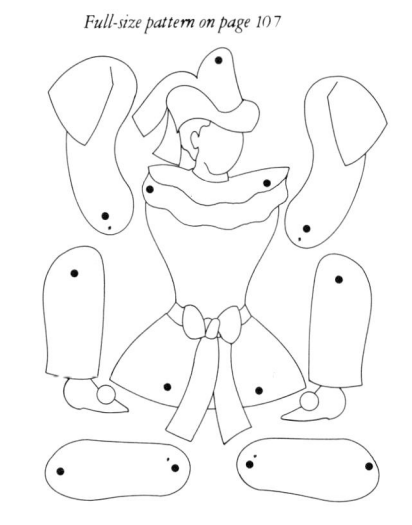

Full-size pattern on page 107

57

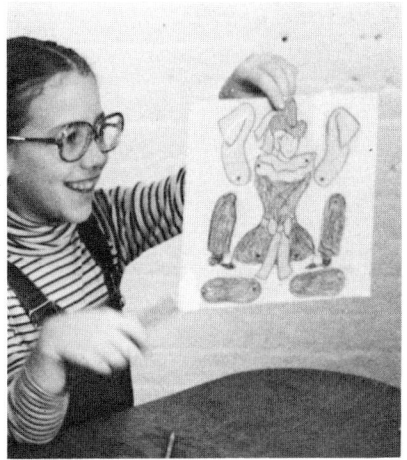

PEDDLER DOLL

*Courtesy of The New-York
Historical Society,
New York City*

"Trinkets for sale! Watches and pincushions, ribbons and necklaces, trinkets for sale!" The peddler sold her wares on the streets of London and traveled across the English countryside selling notions—small decorations and necessities. The customer was never sure just what would be in the peddler's tray, but it was always fun to look at her wares. It was fun, too, to make models of the peddler, and many Victorian Englishwomen made peddler dolls, complete with trays of miniature-sized trinkets (some of which were undoubtedly purchased from real peddlers).

These dolls were nicknamed Notion Nannies. Real peddlers were sometimes young, and many were men, but most Notion Nannies, including the doll pictured here, portrayed the peddler as an old woman, dressed in a bonnet or hood, a cape, and an apron. They were made from wax, wood, and china, and there is even an example of a peddler doll whose face was made out of breadcrumbs. Notion Nannies were clothed in scraps of material, and "adorned" with patches instead of jewels.

General Supplies:

A pencil, white chalk, scissors, a ruler, tracing paper, carbon paper, straight pins, masking tape, white glue, paints and a paintbrush, a needle, and thread.

For the peddler's body you will need an 8- or 9-inch-high bottle (14 to 16 ounces) with a tapered neck. Many products—soda, ketchup, cooking oil—come in bottles the right size and shape. Discard the bottle cap, and be sure to wash out and dry the bottle thoroughly before you use it. You will need newspapers, water, wallpaper paste, and a bowl to make papier-mâché for the peddler's head (see page 8), and an 18-inch piece of wire for the arms.

The peddlers wore old, patched clothes that probably didn't match too well, so use fabrics with contrasting colors and patterns. For the dress use a piece of fabric 18 inches long and 14 inches wide; for the apron a piece 14 inches long and 4 inches wide. For the cape use a piece of felt 9 by 12 inches. Gather scraps of different fabrics to use for patches. You will need three pieces of ¼-inch-wide ribbon: one 12 inches long, to belt the dress and apron, and two pieces, each 6 inches long, to use as ties for the cape. For the bonnet, use a piece of felt 3½ inches by 6 inches, and an 8-inch strip of lace or white fabric that is ½ inch wide. For the tray you will need a 3-by-4-inch piece of cardboard and a 12-inch piece of string. You will need yarn or a wad of cotton for the peddler's hair, and trinkets for the tray. Check around your house to see what you can come up with: buttons, buckles, pieces from discarded costume jewelry, needles, straight pins, safety pins, crayons, pencil stubs, thimbles, small spools of thread, shoelaces. Roll some brightly colored yarn into a small ball, string some tiny beads together into a necklace. Fold and staple tiny pieces of colored paper together to make a book, sew a small pouch, make some paper flowers (see page 24, steps 15 through 19). Small toys or pieces from old games make good wares—so do dolls' clothes. Your local five-and-ten or household goods store is a good place to buy extra inexpensive items to stock the tray.

1. To make the peddler's head, roll a piece of newspaper into a ball approximately 2 inches in diameter. Use masking tape to hold the shape.

2. Place the ball over the bottle opening and tape it to the neck.

3. Prepare the wallpaper-paste mixture and cover the entire ball with one layer of papier-mâché. Layer some papier-mâché from the ball down the neck of the bottle, too, to secure the head. Make the peddler's face by crumpling small pieces of newspaper to form her nose, mouth, and eyebrows. Glue them on with wallpaper paste.

4. You must wait at least 24 hours, until the papier-mâché is completely dry, before painting the face, so continue to make the rest of the peddler and her costume. To make the arms, hold the wire horizontally at a point about one third down the front of the bottle. (The front is the side with the face.)

5. Wrap the wire around the back of the bottle, crossing the wire once and pulling the ends straight out to each side. Tape the wire against the bottle where it crosses.

6. To make the dress: Fold the 18-by-14-inch fabric into quarters (see page 6) to make a rectangle 9 inches long and 7 inches wide. Measure and cut a ½-inch neckline (see page 7).

7. To make the apron: Fold the 14-by-4-inch fabric into quarters to make a rectangle 7 inches long and 2 inches wide. Measure and cut a ¾-inch neckline.

8. To make the cape: Fold the 9-by-12-inch felt in half from left to right to make a rectangle 9 inches long and 6 inches wide. Make a tracing-paper pattern of the cape (see page 10). Line up the fold of the fabric with the pattern according to the instructions on the pattern, and pin the pattern to the felt. Trace around the pattern and cut out the cape, through both layers of felt.

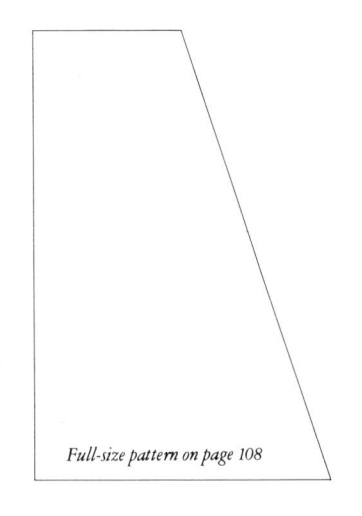

Full-size pattern on page 108

Full-size pattern on page 109

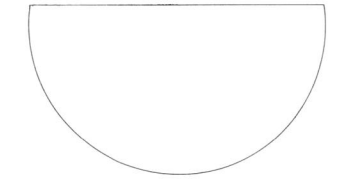

9. Open up the felt. Sew the end of one piece of 6-inch ribbon to each side of the neckline. Sew patches on the cape.

10. To make the bonnet: Make a tracing-paper pattern of the bonnet. Trace the pattern onto the 3½-by-6-inch felt and cut it out.

11. Use a running stitch (see page 5) to gather the back edge of the bonnet. Do the same with the strip of lace.

12. Sew the gathered strip of lace around the brim of the bonnet.

13. To make the peddler's tray: Make a tracing-paper pattern of the tray (see page 10). Trace the tray onto the cardboard. Use carbon paper and trace the two dots and the broken lines. Cut out the tray.

14. Fold the two long strips in toward the middle of the tray along the broken lines. Let them each stand up straight.

15. Do the same with the shorter strips. Tape the side edges of the strips together at each of the four corners.

16. Use the point of the scissors to make two holes through the dots.

17. Paint the tray inside and out. When the paint is dry, put one end of the 12-inch string through one of the holes—from the outside to the inside—and tape it to the inside of the tray. Put the other end of the string through the other hole and tape it to the inside of the tray.

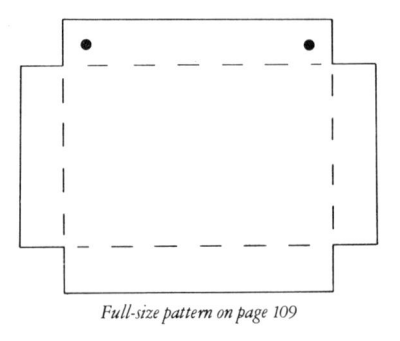

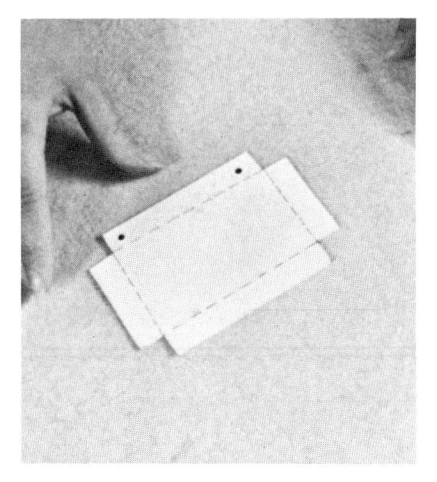

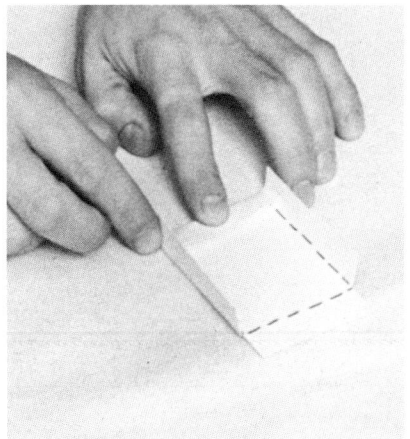

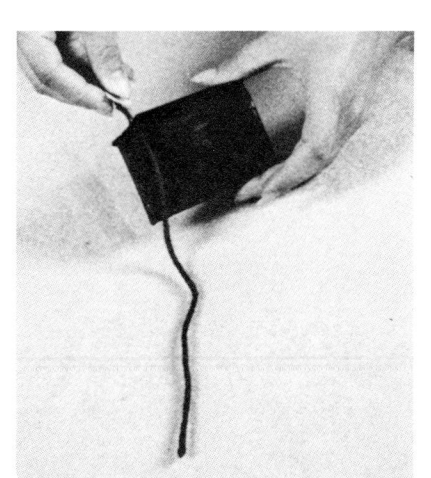

Full-size pattern on page 109

18. After the papier-mâché has dried, paint the peddler's face. Glue yarn or cotton to the top of her head for hair.

19. To assemble the peddler, put the dress on over her head. Use a running stitch (see page 5) to gather the neckline of the dress tightly around the doll's neck to hold it in place.

20. Put the apron on over the dress. Put the 12-inch ribbon around her waist, as a belt, tying it in a bow in the back. Pull the wire arms through the sleeves of the dress.

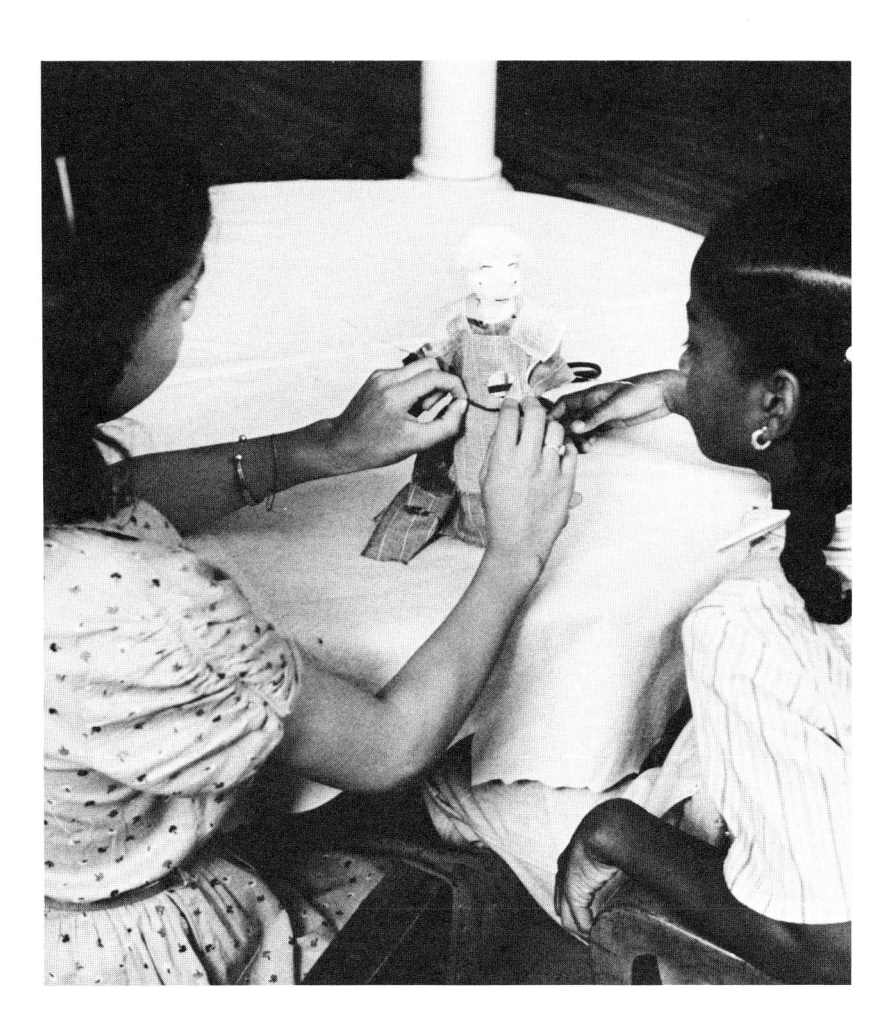

21. Dab a small amount of white glue around the inside of the back edge of the bonnet. Put the bonnet on the peddler's head and press the back edge against her neck to glue it in place.

22. Put the tray on over the peddler's head. To hold the tray up in front of her body, bend and tape the ends of her wire arms under the front of the tray.

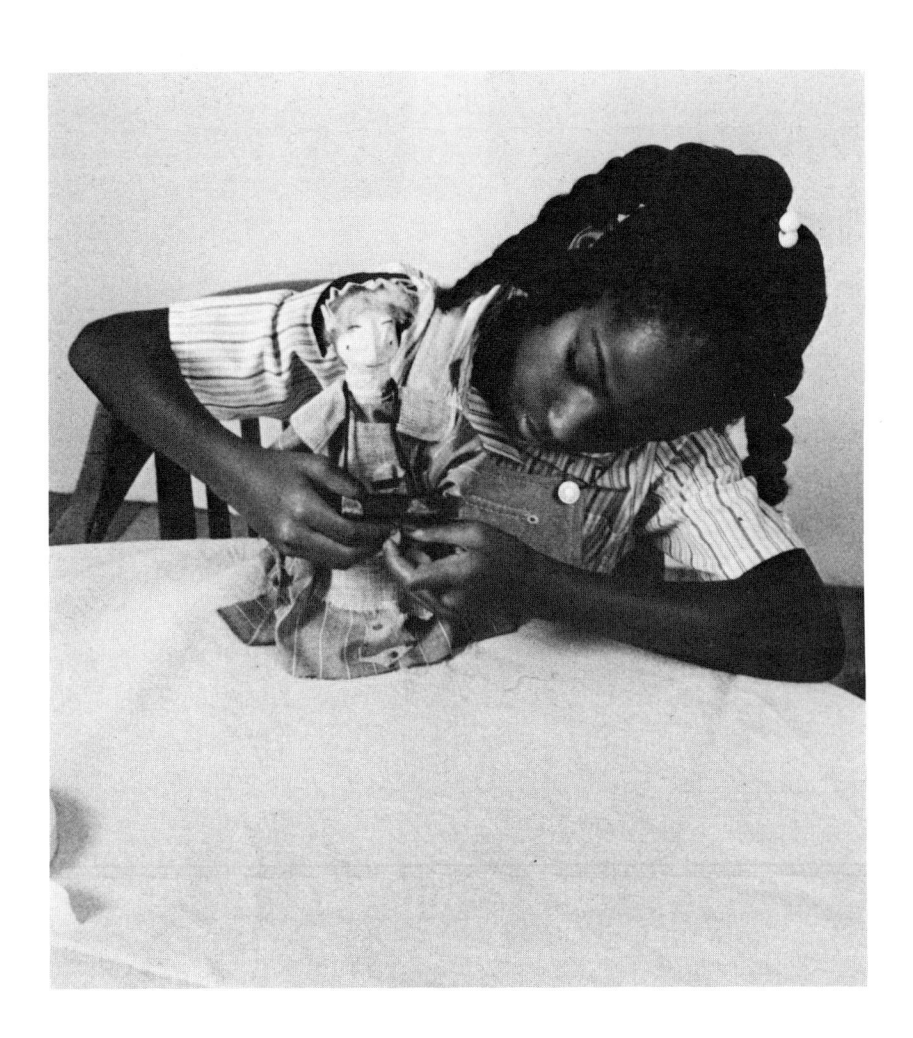

23. Stock her tray with wares. Try various arrangements—remember, her tray should look inviting, and not too neat. You can glue the wares in place, or leave them loose, so you can play with them.

24. Tie the cape around the peddler's shoulders.

25. Real peddlers displayed their names on city vendors' licenses. You can make a little sign with your name and the date and attach it to the tray, or the bottom of the peddler's dress.

PERUVIAN DOLL

Courtesy of American Museum of Natural History

In many parts of the world, grass and even leaves are used to make dolls. In Malaya, dolls were made from strips of palm leaves, and the Mojave Indians of southern California made small clay baby dolls and wrapped them in grass "blankets."

In Peru doll makers used reed, a tall, sturdy grass. The reed was folded and tied to make a simple stick figure. Then a small sack was stuffed for the doll's head, and its arms and legs were wrapped in yarn. Peruvians are expert weavers, and a doll usually was dressed in a poncho, the blanketlike woven shirt that is the costume worn by most Peruvian men and women.

The doll pictured here and others like him were found buried in graves, and we think they were offerings to the dead. Some of the dolls are over five hundred years old, but because Peru is a dry country, and the dolls were buried underground, they were in almost perfect condition when they were found.

General Supplies:

A pencil or white chalk, a ruler, scissors, masking tape, paint and a paintbrush, newspapers, a piece of cardboard approximately 12 inches long, a needle, and thread.

To make the frame of the doll you will need, in place of reeds, one piece of wire 24 inches long, and another 9 inches long. You will also need cotton, cotton batting, gauze, or strips of material to pad the frame. You will need a piece of 12-by-6-inch fabric for the poncho, and another piece, 9 by 4 inches, for the cloth sack that forms the doll's head. For each, choose a textured fabric like burlap or terry cloth, to imitate woven Peruvian cloth. You will also need yarn of two different colors.

1. Fold the 24-inch piece of wire in half. Hold the wire upright, with the fold at the top.

2. To make the doll's legs, measure 8 inches down from the top of the wire. Wrap a piece of masking tape around the two thicknesses of wire at this point.

3. Gently separate the bottom ends of the wire.

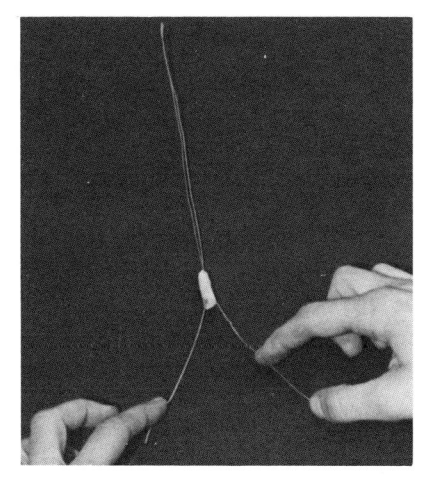

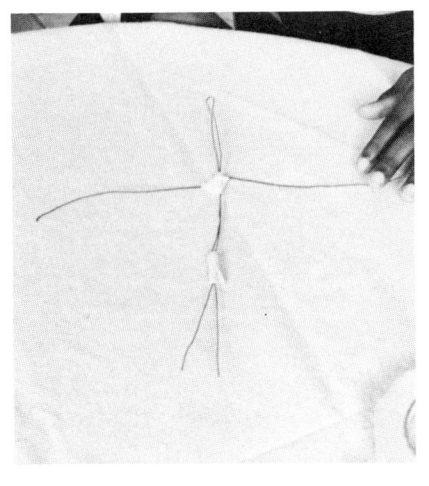

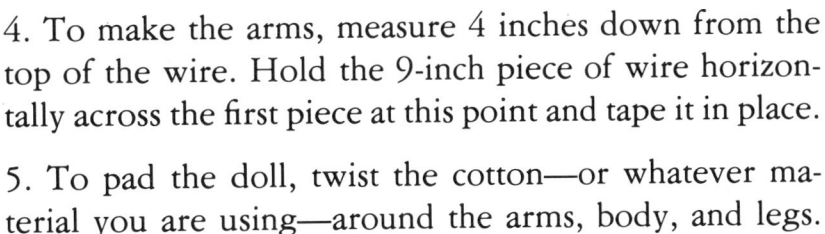

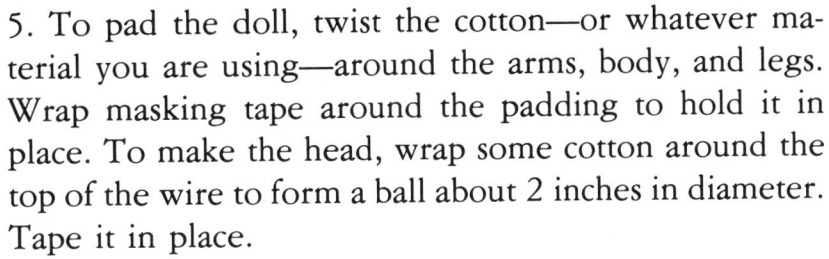

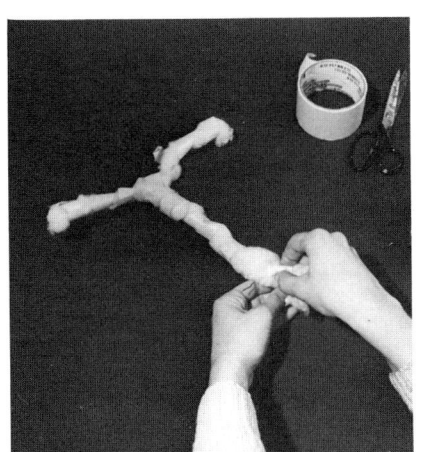

4. To make the arms, measure 4 inches down from the top of the wire. Hold the 9-inch piece of wire horizontally across the first piece at this point and tape it in place.

5. To pad the doll, twist the cotton—or whatever material you are using—around the arms, body, and legs. Wrap masking tape around the padding to hold it in place. To make the head, wrap some cotton around the top of the wire to form a ball about 2 inches in diameter. Tape it in place.

6. To cover the padding, cut 36-inch pieces of two different colors of yarn. Tie the ends of both pieces of yarn to the end of one of the doll's arms. Spiral both pieces of yarn around the padding together, wrapping it securely, but not so tightly that the padding pops through.

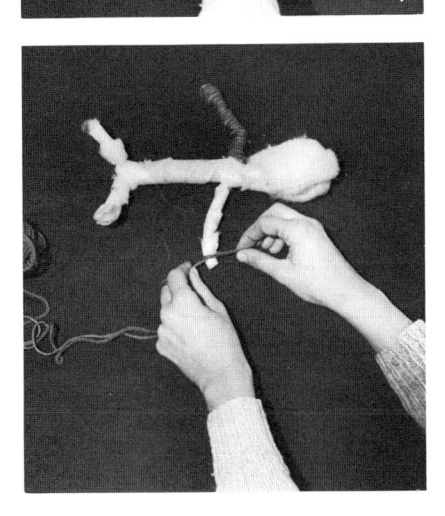

7. Wrap the whole arm. Tie the two ends of the yarn together in a knot at the doll's shoulder, to hold the padding in place. Wrap the other arm. Using the same method, wrap each leg with two 36-inch pieces of yarn. You don't need to wrap the body or the head.

8. To make the poncho: Fold the 12-by-6-inch fabric into quarters (see page 6) to make a rectangle 6 inches long and 3 inches wide. Measure and cut a ½-inch neckline (see page 7). Open the poncho, lay it flat on newspapers to protect your work surface, and decorate it by painting geometric designs on the front and the back. It is sometimes hard to paint on textured fabric, so the paint will have to be fairly thick. Put the poncho on over the doll's head.

9. To make the cloth sack that covers his head, fold the 9-by-4-inch fabric in half to make a rectangle 4½ inches long and 4 inches wide. The fold in the fabric should be at the top. Place a piece of newspaper between the two layers of fabric to prevent the paint from bleeding

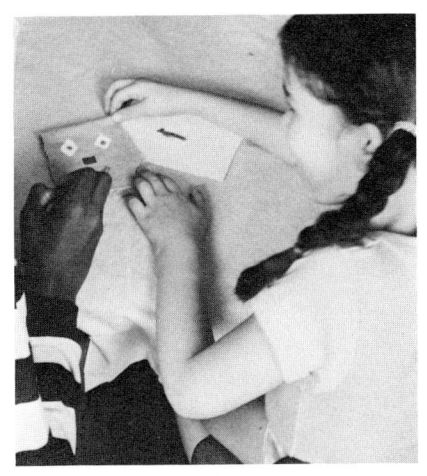

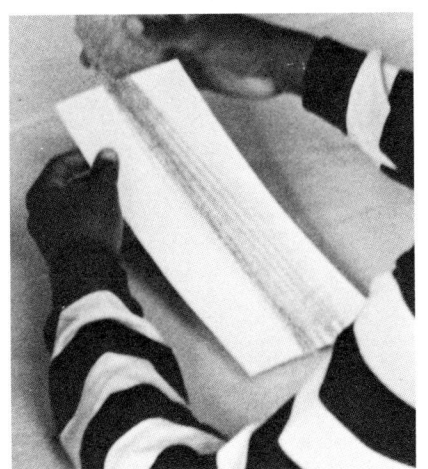

through. Draw the doll's face in pencil or chalk. Use simple geometric shapes, like diamonds or ovals for eyes, a square for a nose, and a line or a circle for the mouth. Paint in the doll's features, and for extra emphasis stitch around them with colored yarn when the paint is dry. Sew the front and the back of the folded fabric together along each side. Leave the bottom edge open.

10. To make the hair: Wrap yarn around the length of the cardboard about a dozen times.

11. Slide the loops of wrapped yarn off the cardboard.

12. Pinch the loops together in the center. Use a piece of yarn 6 inches long to tie them together around the middle. Cut through the looped ends of the yarn. With a stitch or two, sew the hair in place to the center of the top of the sack.

13. Put the sack on over the doll's head. Use a running stitch (see page 5) to gather the open end of the sack tightly around the doll's neck to hold it in place.

ZULU DOLL

*Courtesy Brooklyn
Children's Museum*

This mother and the baby she carries on her back were made by the Zulu people in Africa. When the first dolls of this type were made, hundreds of years ago, the bodies (which you can't see because they are covered by fabric) were fashioned around the tiny dried shells of a fruit called a gourd. The dolls were given to young girls, who played with them, acting out scenes of a mother taking care of her baby. The dolls are still being made today, but now a piece of cardboard or a small tin can is used for the body. The Zulus, who place great importance on their daughters' learning to become good mothers, still give them to little girls. And some of these dolls are sold to tourists as souvenirs.

The mother wears a popular African hairdo, the topknot. The glass beads, used to represent her eyes, nose, and mouth and wrapped around her entire body, were common trade items in Africa, and often used to decorate clothing.

General Supplies:

Scissors, masking tape, white glue, a needle, and thread.

For the doll's body you will need an empty 14- to 16-ounce can, which is about 4 inches high. Corn, tomatoes, juice—many different food products come in cans this size. Be sure to wash out and dry the can thoroughly before you use it. You will need a strip of cardboard ¼ inch wide by 8 inches long. To cover the can and form the doll's head use a dark-colored fabric such as denim, 28 inches long and 8 inches wide. You will need a smaller piece of the same kind of fabric, 4 inches long and 1½ inches wide, to make the baby's pouch. You will need dark-colored yarn, scraps of fabric to stuff the doll's head with, and beads to stitch around the doll's body. You can buy small colored beads at a craft supply store and string them together on long pieces of thread, or buy about 10 yards of colored sequins at a sewing store. The advantage of using sequins is that they are already strung together. In place of either, use ribbon or colored cord. You can buy rolls of colored cord at most stationery stores. If you use ribbon or cord, you will still need a few beads, or buttons or sequins, for the doll's eyes, nose, and mouth. You will also need two small sticks or pencil stubs, each about 3 inches long.

1. Hold the can upright, with the open end up. To make the doll's arms, tape the strip of cardboard across the middle of the top of the can. An equal amount of cardboard should overlap the can at each edge.

2. To make a bag that will cover the can and form the doll's head, fold the large piece of fabric in half from top to bottom to make a rectangle 14 inches long and 8 inches wide. Sew the front and the back of the bag together along the 14-inch sides. Leave the 8-inch side unsewn.

3. Put the can in the bag so the bottom of the can sits on the fold.

4. Tie a piece of yarn around the bag, just above the top of the can, to form the doll's head.

5. Gather the fabric around the end of one cardboard arm and tie it in place with a piece of yarn. Repeat this with the other cardboard arm.

6. Tie a piece of yarn around the bag just under the arms, to hold the fabric in place against the can.

7. To make the head, stuff the top of the bag with scraps of fabric. Use a running stitch to gather the open top edges together (see page 5) into a rounded shape.

8. Wrap strings of beads around the body and arms to cover the fabric. Stitch them in place around the doll.

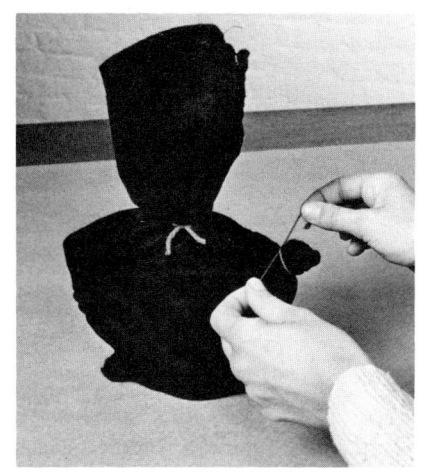

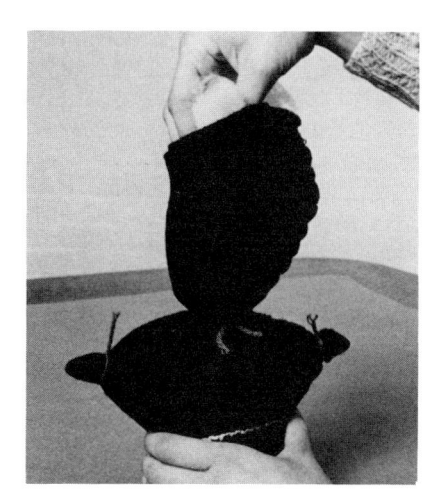

9. Outline the round shape of the head with sequins, and glue sequins, beads, or buttons on for the doll's eyes, nose, and mouth.

10. To make the topknot, push one of the sticks or pencil stubs down into the top of the head—there should be an opening between a couple of stitches for you to do this, or you can use the point of the scissors to make a small opening in the fabric. Push the stick in about ½ inch so it is secure. Glue beads or sequins all over the stick.

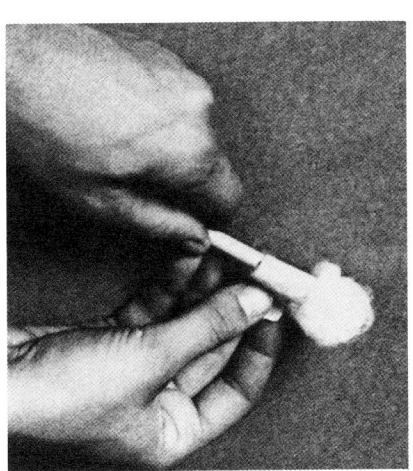

11. To make the baby: Tape a wad of cotton or a scrap of fabric to one end of the other stick or pencil stub—this will form the baby's head. Glue sequins or beads around the head and body.

12. To make the baby's pouch: Fold the 4-by-1½-inch fabric in half from top to bottom to make a 2-by-1½ inch rectangle. Sew the front and the back of the fabric together along the 2-inch sides.

13. Use the point of the scissors to make a small hole in each corner of the open top of the pouch.

14. Cut a piece of yarn 12 inches long. Slip one end of the yarn through each hole and tie the ends together.

15. Slip the baby into the pouch. Hang the yarn around the mother doll's neck so the pouch rests on her back.

KACHINA BUTTERFLY MAIDEN

Courtesy of American Museum of Natural History

The Hopi Indians, of the southwestern United States, believe in supernatural messengers, called Kachinas, sent by the gods. Kachinas represent the many spirits of the Hopi world. There are Kachinas for crops, plants, and even animals, but most of the Kachinas represent the elements—air, earth, rain, and wind. Since the Kachinas are spirits, they don't have bodies. So the Hopis stage elaborate ceremonies, dress up in masks and costumes, and "lend" their bodies to the Kachinas for their visits to the village. They sing and dance as they wait for the spirits to come, and as part of the ritual, wooden Kachina figures are given to the children of the tribe.

Although they are played with, Kachinas are not meant to be toys; they help children learn the names and stories of the more than 300 different Kachinas. The figures are carved and painted by special sculptors. They are not realistic-looking, for Kachinas are not human, but special designs are used to represent each Kachina. The one shown here is the Polik Mana, or Butterfly Maiden, and she is identified by her distinctive "stepped" headdress.

General Supplies:

A pencil, a ruler, scissors, tracing paper, carbon paper, masking tape, paint and a paintbrush, white glue.

You can make the Butterfly Maiden out of Styrofoam, which can be bought in most art and craft supply stores and some five-and-tens. Use a ball approximately 2 to 3 inches in diameter for the head and a 4-inch-high cone for the body. In place of Styrofoam you can roll newspaper into a ball for the head and use two cone-shaped paper cups for the body. Stack the cups one inside the other so they are strong enough to support the head. Or you can make a tracing-paper pattern (see page 10) of the cone shape, trace it onto 9-by-5-inch cardboard, cut it out, roll it into a cone, overlap the edges slightly, and tape it. You will need newspaper, water, wallpaper paste, and a bowl for papier-mâché; a piece of cardboard 6 by 8 inches; colored yarn; and some feathers. You can buy feathers at a craft supply store, get them from a pet shop, or make them out of construction paper.

1. Tape the ball to the top of the cone.

2. To make the headdress: Make a tracing-paper pattern of the stepped shape (see page 10). Trace the shape onto cardboard and use carbon paper to trace the broken line. Cut out the shape. Repeat this four more times so you have five cutout pieces in all.

3. Fold the tabs along the broken lines. Attach the stepped shapes to make a frame for the face by taping the tabs around the top and sides of the ball.

4. Prepare the wallpaper-paste mixture (see page 8) and cover the entire ball and cone with one layer of papier-mâché. Papier-mâché the tape holding the tabs, but do not papier-mâché the headdress.

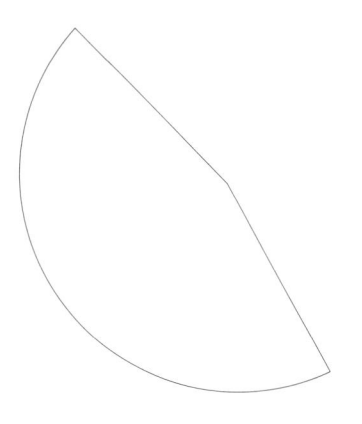

Full-size patterns on pages 99, 109

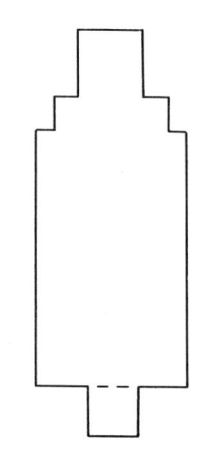

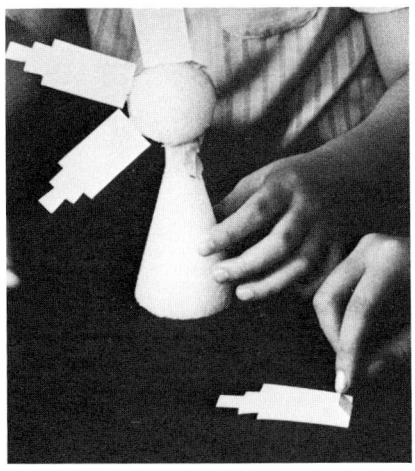

5. Wait 24 hours, and when the papier-mâché is totally dry, paint the face and headdress a light color. Draw simple geometric shapes such as triangles, squares, and circles to decorate the headdress and to make the Kachina's eyes, nose, and mouth. Paint the shapes. Paint the cone two different colors so it looks like the Kachina has a blanket—or a tablita, as the Indians call it—wrapped around her shoulders.

6. To make each of the three fluffy yarn balls that decorate the Kachina's costume: Wrap yarn around your four outstretched fingers about a dozen times.

7. Slide the loops of wrapped yarn off your hand.

8. Pinch the loops together in the center. Use a piece of yarn about 6 inches long to tie them together around the middle. Cut through the looped ends of the yarn. Repeat steps 7 and 8 twice more to make three balls.

9. Glue one ball in place at the Kachina's neck, and glue the other two to the bottom of the front of her costume.

10. Glue feathers around the top of the headdress.

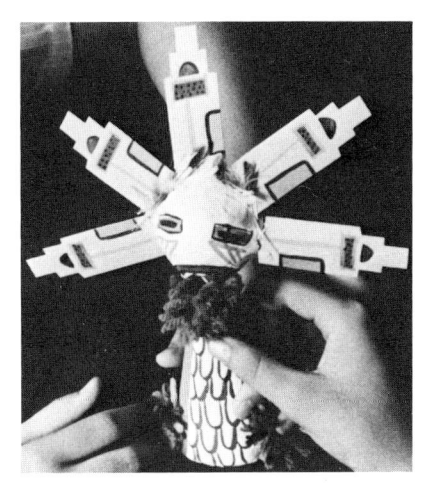

SUDANESE BRIDE DOLL

*Courtesy Brooklyn
Children's Museum*

In the Sudan, which is south of the Sahara Desert, children call dolls "aroussas," the Arabic word for bride. Not all the dolls Sudanese children play with are bride dolls, of course, but this one is.

The doll is made from soft cloth and has a long neck and stumpy arms. She is decorated with bands of ribbon and numerous buttons, beads, and sequins. It is traditional that on their wedding day Sudanese girls adorn themselves with all the jewelry they own, and as much as they can borrow from friends. This doll is dressed as elaborately as a Sudanese bride would be. Even the wide-brimmed hat she wears has trinkets dangling down.

General Supplies:

A pencil, scissors, tracing paper, straight pins, a needle, and thread.

You will need a piece of felt approximately 12 inches square, to make the doll, and cotton batting or scraps of fabric to stuff it. For the hat you will need a piece of cardboard 5 by 3½ inches, and a 6-inch square of dark felt or other fabric. You will need ribbon and ornaments to decorate the doll. Collect an interesting assortment of jewels from discarded costume jewelry; beads, buttons, and sequins from the five-and-ten; metal washers, nuts, even small nails from the hardware store.

1. Make a tracing paper pattern (see page 10) of the doll. Trace two patterns onto the felt, one for the back, the other for the front, and cut them out.

2. Lay out one piece (this will be the back of the doll). Pile cotton batting or scraps of fabric on top of this piece, so the stuffing is about ½ inch thick.

3. Place the front of the doll on top of the stuffing, line

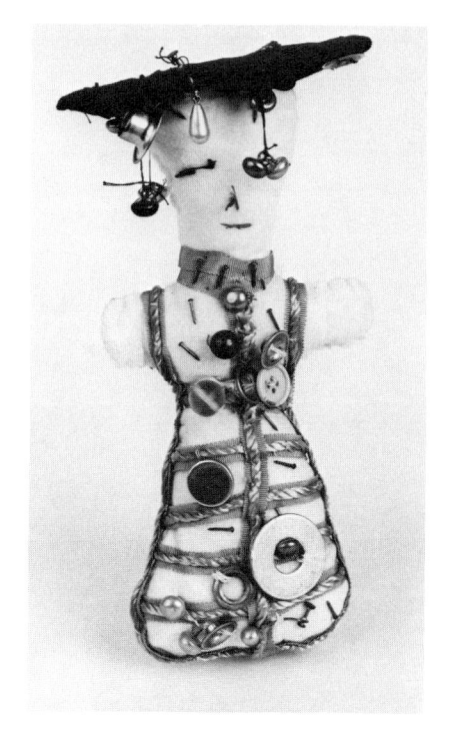

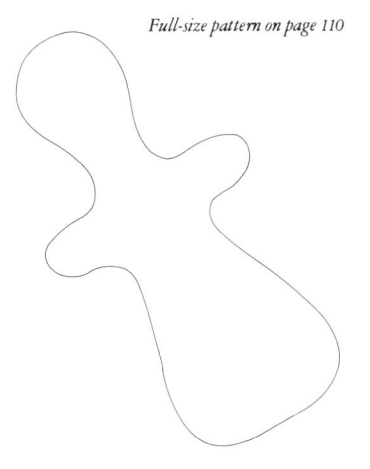

Full-size pattern on page 110

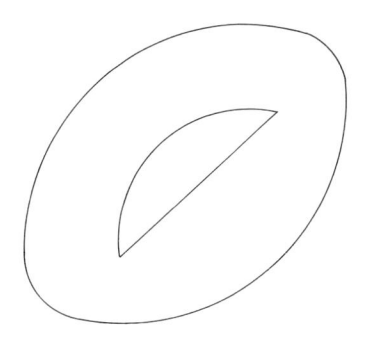

Full-size pattern on page 111

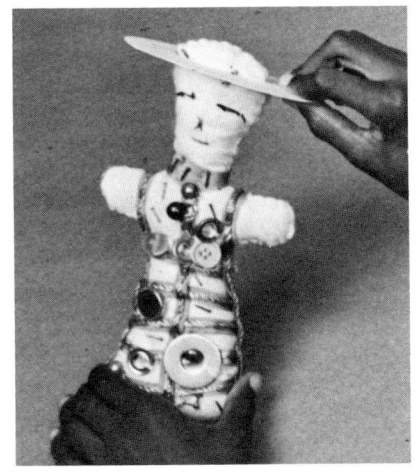

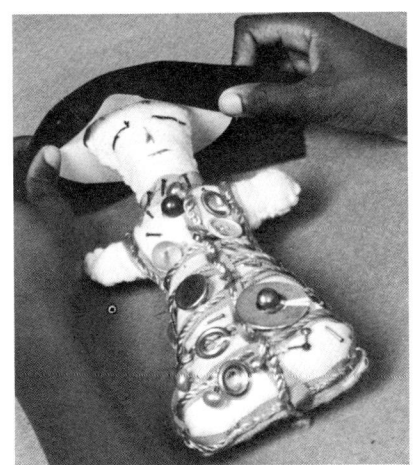

up the edges of the front and back of the doll, and use an overcast stitch (see page 2) to sew them together around the entire shape.

4. Use the pencil to draw in the doll's face, and stitch over your pencil lines with colored thread.

5. To decorate the doll, take ribbon and wrap it in a crisscross pattern around the front and back of the body, and stitch it in place. Sew a band of ribbon around her neck. Sew sequins, buttons, beads, and ornaments over her entire body.

6. To make the hat: Make a tracing-paper pattern of the hat (see page 7). Trace it onto cardboard. Use carbon paper to trace the slit. Cut out the hat and the center slit.

7. Put the top of the doll's head through the center slit so the hat sits securely on her head.

8. Wrap the piece of fabric over the top of the hat, folding the edges under the brim. Sew through the fabric and cardboard, using a few stitches where needed to hold the fabric in place.

9. To hang beads from the hat, thread a needle with a piece of thread about 6 to 8 inches long. Knot the end of the thread. Poke the needle through the hat near the edge, from the top down, and pull the thread all the way through.

10. Put the needle and thread through a bead, a button, or any ornament with a hole. Cut off the needle and tie the ornament to the end of the thread. Repeat this in several places around the edge of the hat, so you have lots of beads and sequins hanging down.

FORTUNE-TELLING DOLL

Courtesy of The New-York Historical Society, New York City

Ouija boards, crystal balls, tarot cards, messages tucked inside Chinese fortune cookies—whether or not you believe it's possible to predict the future, it's fun to play fortune-telling games. In the eighteenth and nineteenth centuries people had a special fortune-telling game of their own they played with a doll.

Like the peddler doll, this one was patterned after a real character, the professional fortune-teller who traveled from town to town claiming to predict the future. The dolls themselves became popular playthings, and even Queen Victoria had one.

The fortune-teller doll has a wooden body. Her hair and makeup, and even the top of her dress, make her look like an old-fashioned lady, but her skirt is certainly different: Hidden between its folds are fortunes—open one of these petals and "your fate will be revealed."

General Supplies:

A pencil, white chalk, a ruler, scissors, tracing paper, carbon paper, straight pins, masking tape, white glue, paint and a paintbrush, a needle, and thread.

For the head and body of the fortune-teller you will need a strip of wood 12 inches long by 1 to 1½ inches wide. Paint stirrers, which you can get at most hardware or paint stores, are perfect because one end of the stirrer is slightly rounded, and it naturally suggests the doll's head. Instead of a paint stirrer you can use balsa wood, available at hobby or craft stores, or heavy cardboard. You will also need a ½-inch-wide strip of wood or cardboard 9½ inches long for the arms, and a 4-by-1½-inch piece as a base for the doll to stand on. You can cut balsa wood or cardboard to these dimensions using an ordinary pair of scissors. You will need a dozen pieces of paper to make the petals of the fortune-teller's skirt. Use colored construction paper or regular white writing paper. You will need colored felt-tipped markers, colored pencils, or crayons to write the fortunes with, yarn for the doll's hair, and a piece of fabric 10 inches long and 9 inches wide for the blouse. You can decorate the blouse with lace and ribbon. You will also need some beads for a necklace.

1. Hold the 12-inch strip of wood upright. If you are using a paint stirrer, hold it so the rounded end is at the top.

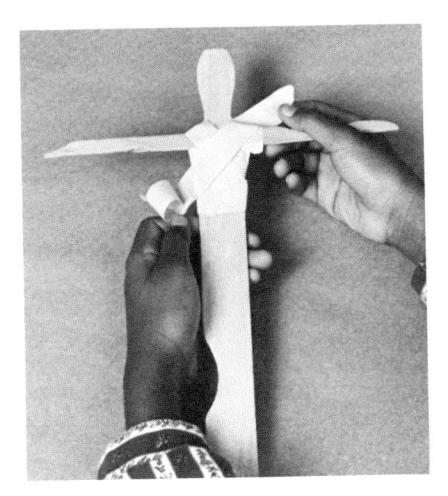

2. To attach the arms, measure about 2 inches down from the top of the strip. Place the 9½-inch strip of cardboard or wood horizontally across the first piece at this point and tape it in place.

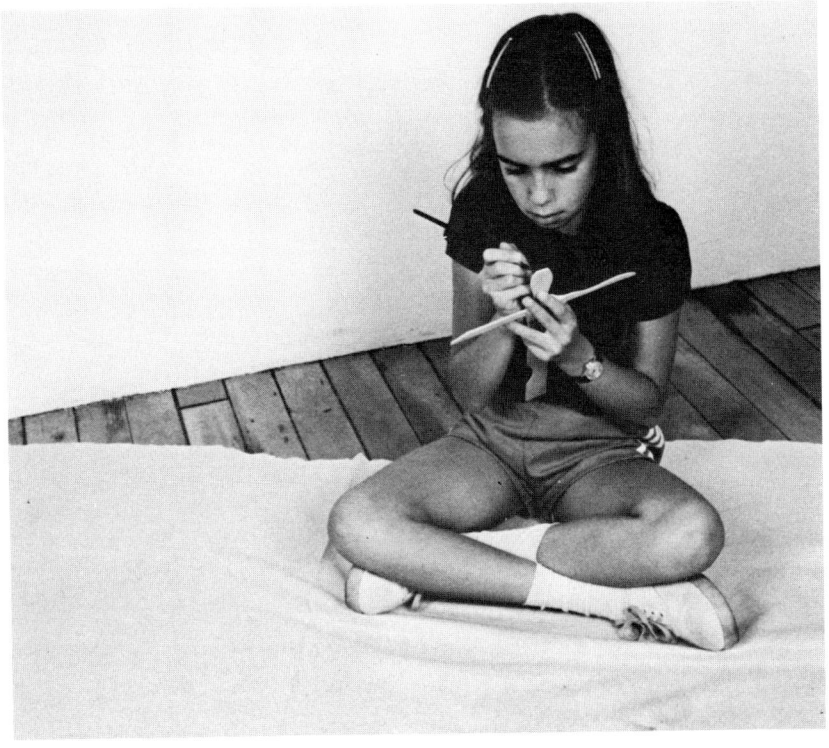

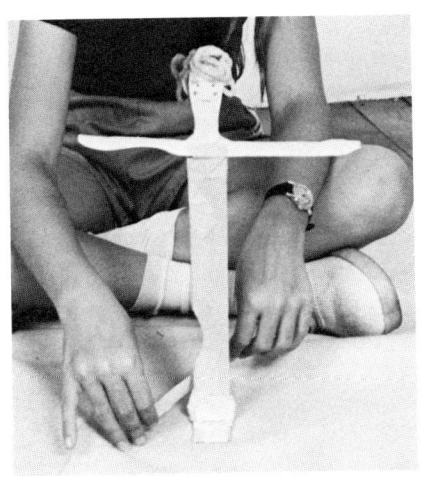

3. Paint the fortune-teller's head, and the front, back, and sides of her neck and arms. It is not necessary to paint the rest of her body, since it will be covered by her costume. Paint on eyes, a nose, and a mouth, and glue on some yarn for her hair.

4. Stand the fortune-teller on the middle of the cardboard or wood base. Use masking tape to tape her in place in this standing position.

5. To make the skirt: Make a tracing-paper pattern (see page 10) of the petal. Trace two petals onto each piece of paper, so you have 24 in all. Use carbon paper and a ruler to trace the broken lines. Cut out the petals.

6. Use different colors and write a prediction on each petal below the broken line. The predictions can be funny, nice, or even scary. Keep them simple, and about one sentence long. For example:

> You will be eaten by a great white shark.
> You will marry a princess.
> You will marry a prince.
> You will turn into a frog.
> Your allowance will be doubled.

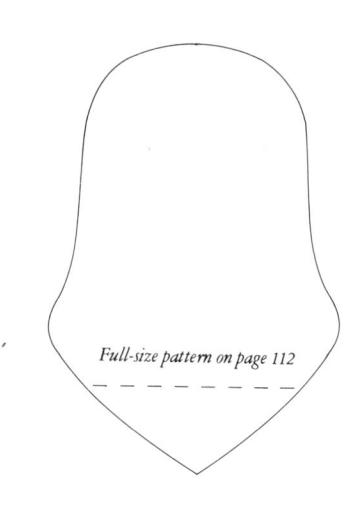

Full-size pattern on page 112

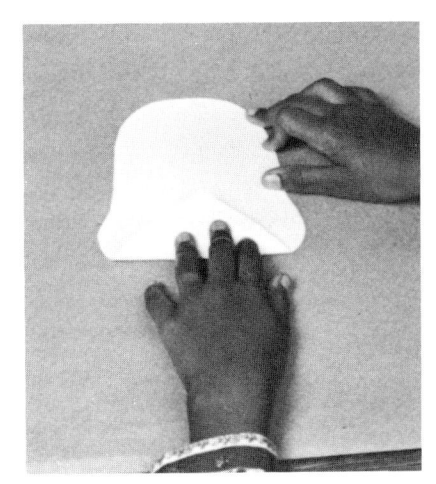

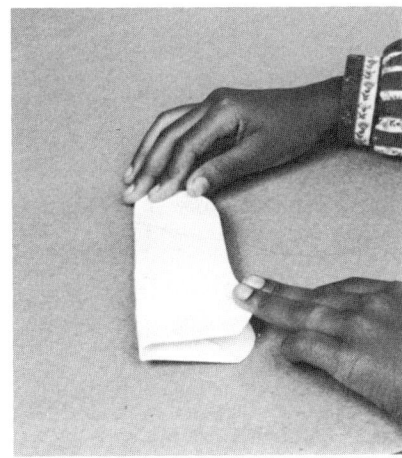

7. To cover up the fortunes, fold the bottom point of each petal up toward the top, along the broken line, with the fortune inside.

8. Then fold each petal in half from left to right.

9. Keep the petals folded. Stack them one on top of the other so all the lengthwise folds are on the left. String the tops of the petals together with a needle and thread.

10. After all the petals are gathered on the thread, position them around the doll's waist and tie the ends of the thread together to make the skirt.

11. To make the blouse: Fold the fabric into quarters (see page 4) to make a rectangle 5 inches long and 4½ inches wide. Make a tracing-paper pattern of the blouse. Line up the fold of the fabric with the pattern according to the instructions on the pattern, and pin the pattern to the fabric. Trace around the pattern. Cutting through all four layers of fabric, cut out the blouse.

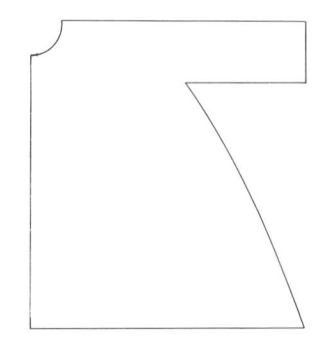

Full-size pattern on page 113

12. Put the blouse on over the fortune-teller's head. Arrange the sleeves over the arms. Sew the front and the back of the blouse together along the undersides of the sleeves and down the sides. Trim the edges with ribbon or lace. Use a running stitch (see page 5) to gather the blouse straight across the front from under one arm to the other.

13. String beads in a necklace around her neck.

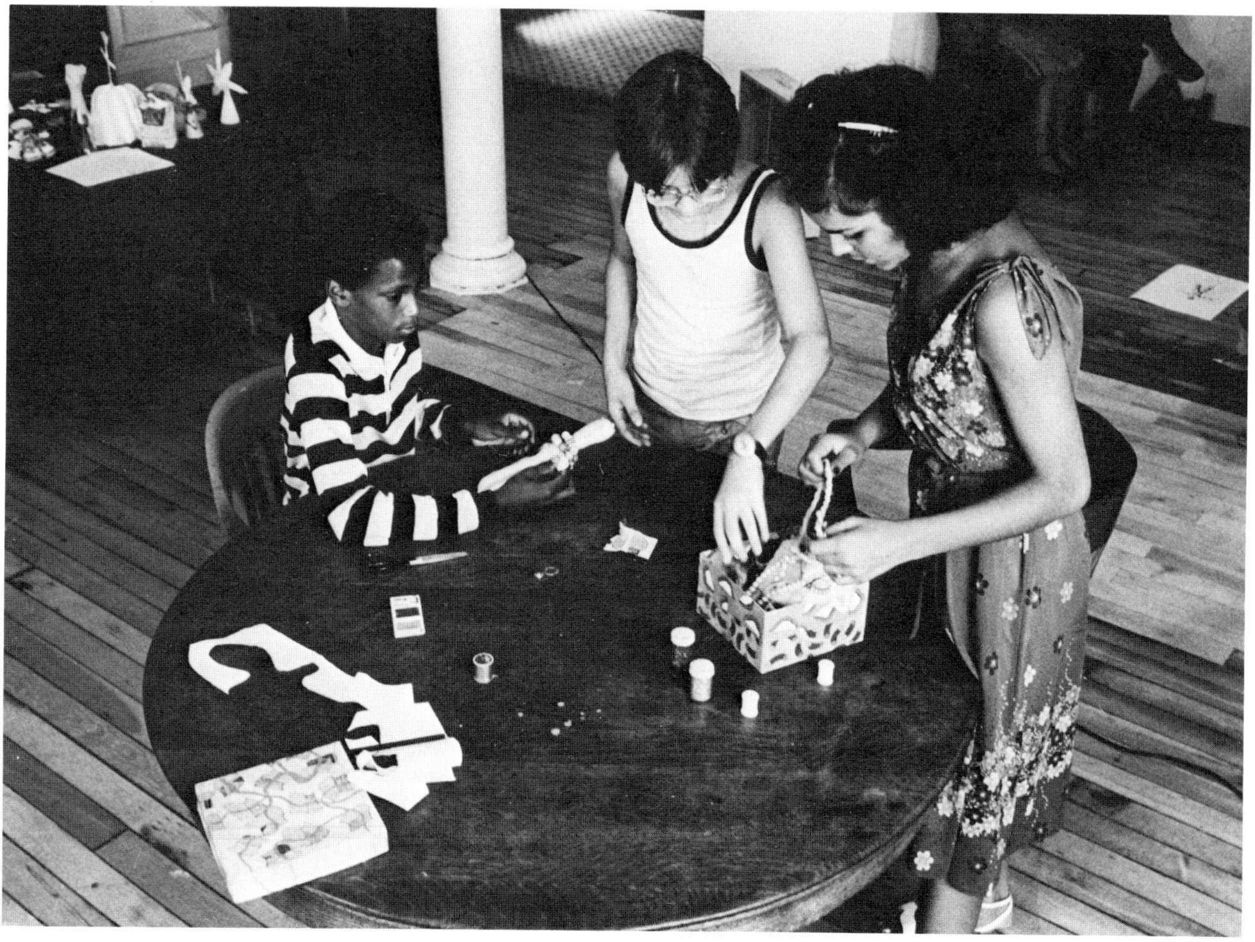

THE PATTERNS

Cone shape

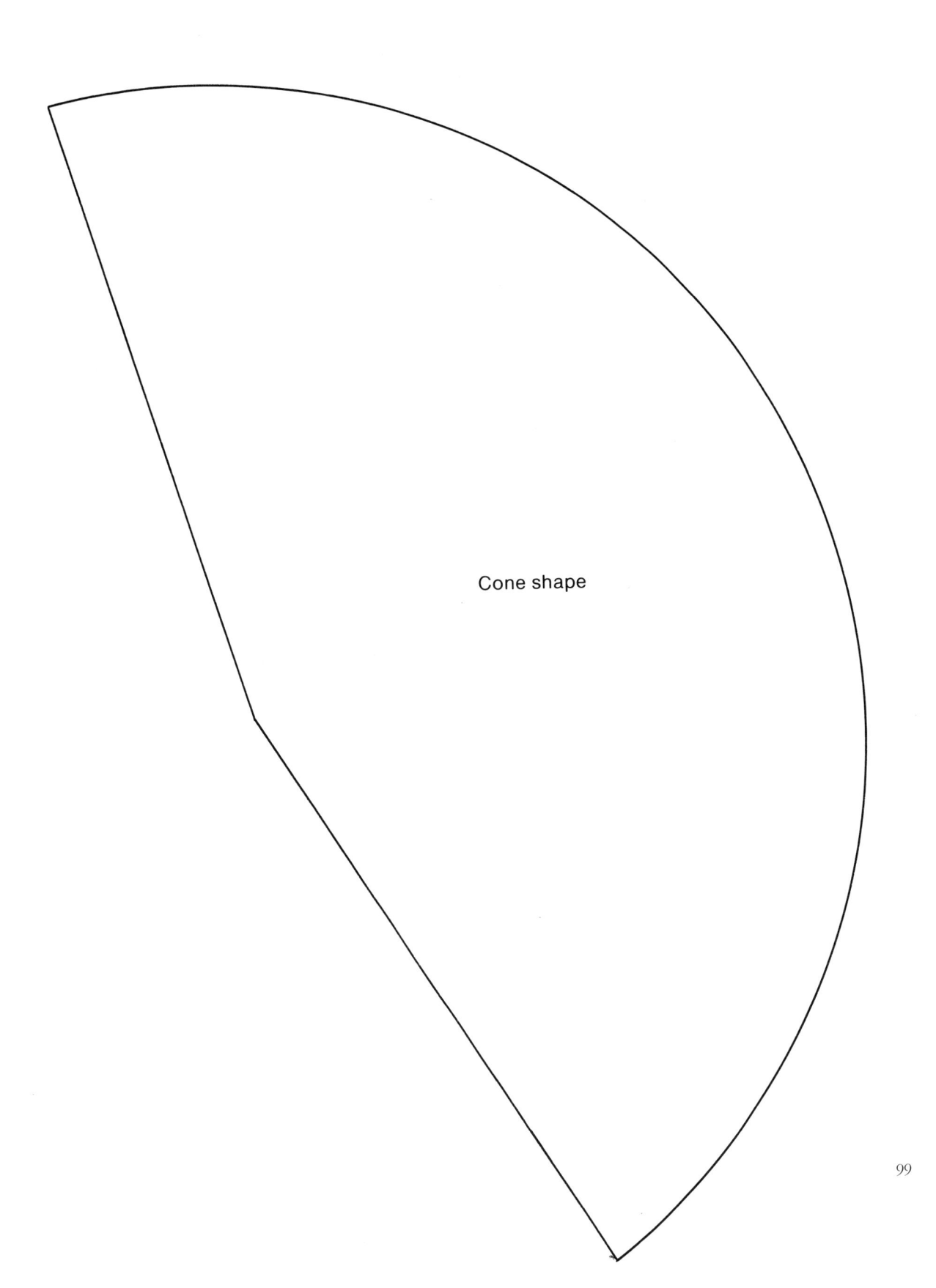

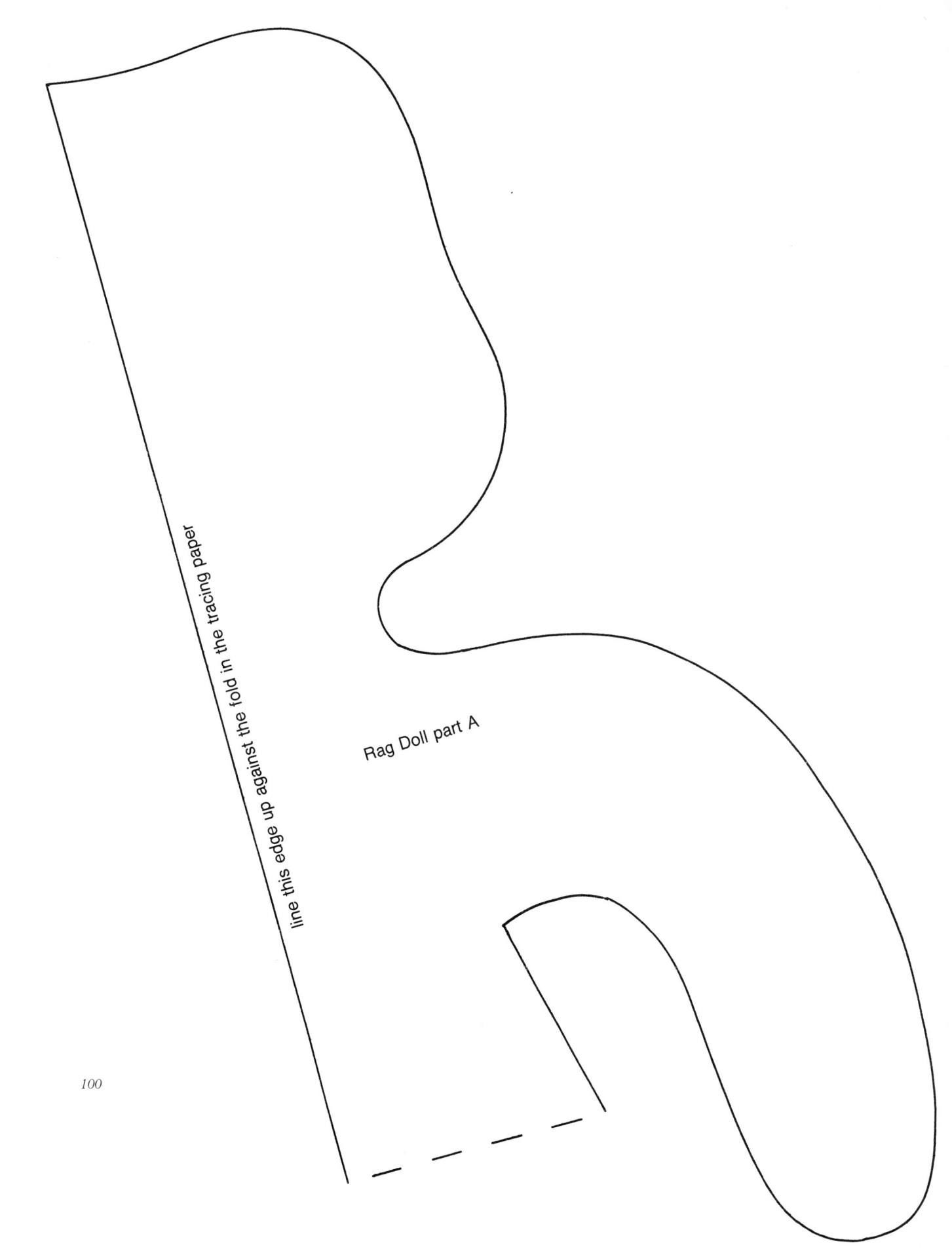

line this edge up against the fold in the tracing paper

Rag Doll part A

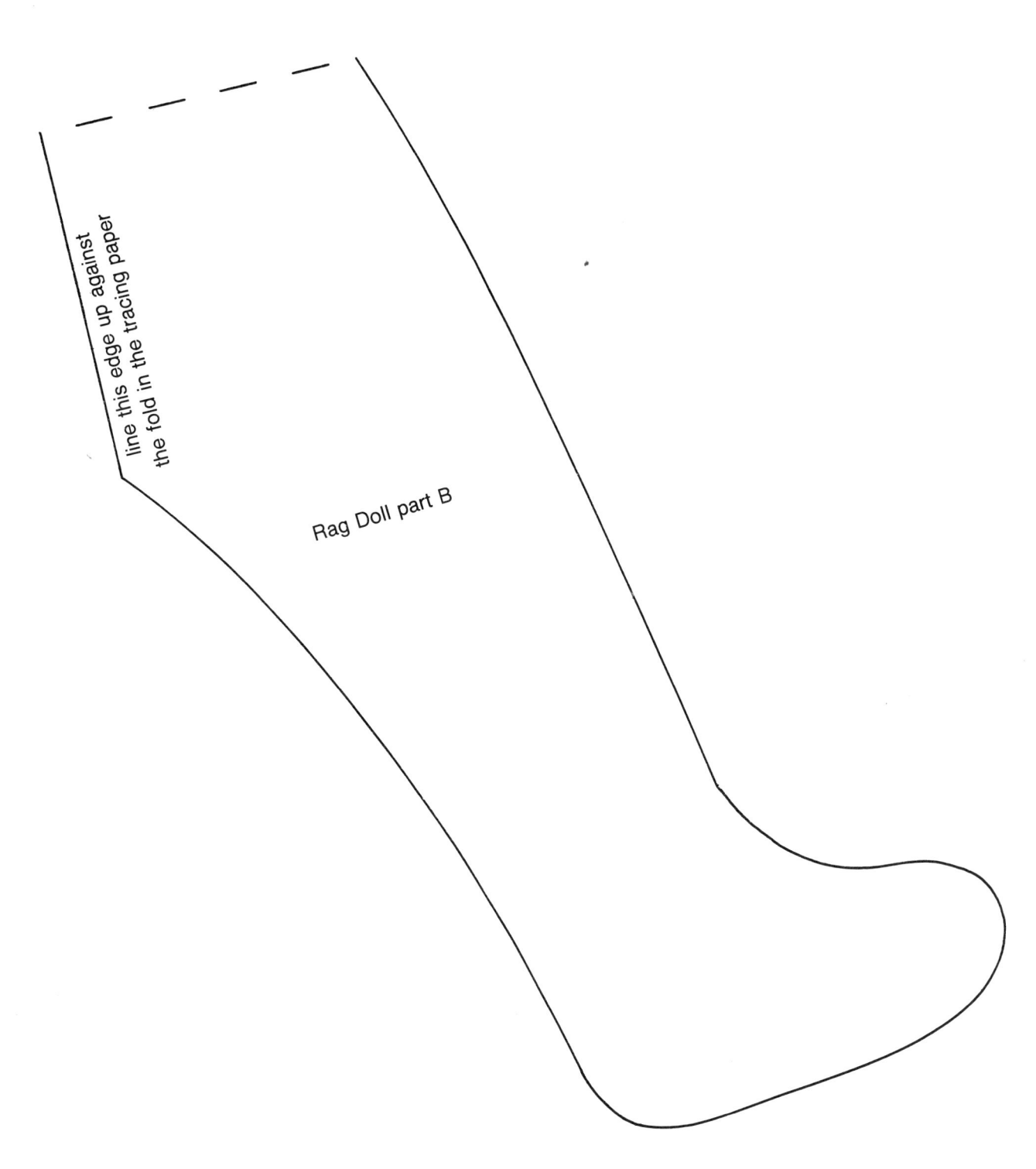

line this edge up against the fold in the tracing paper

Rag Doll part B

Rag Doll Dress

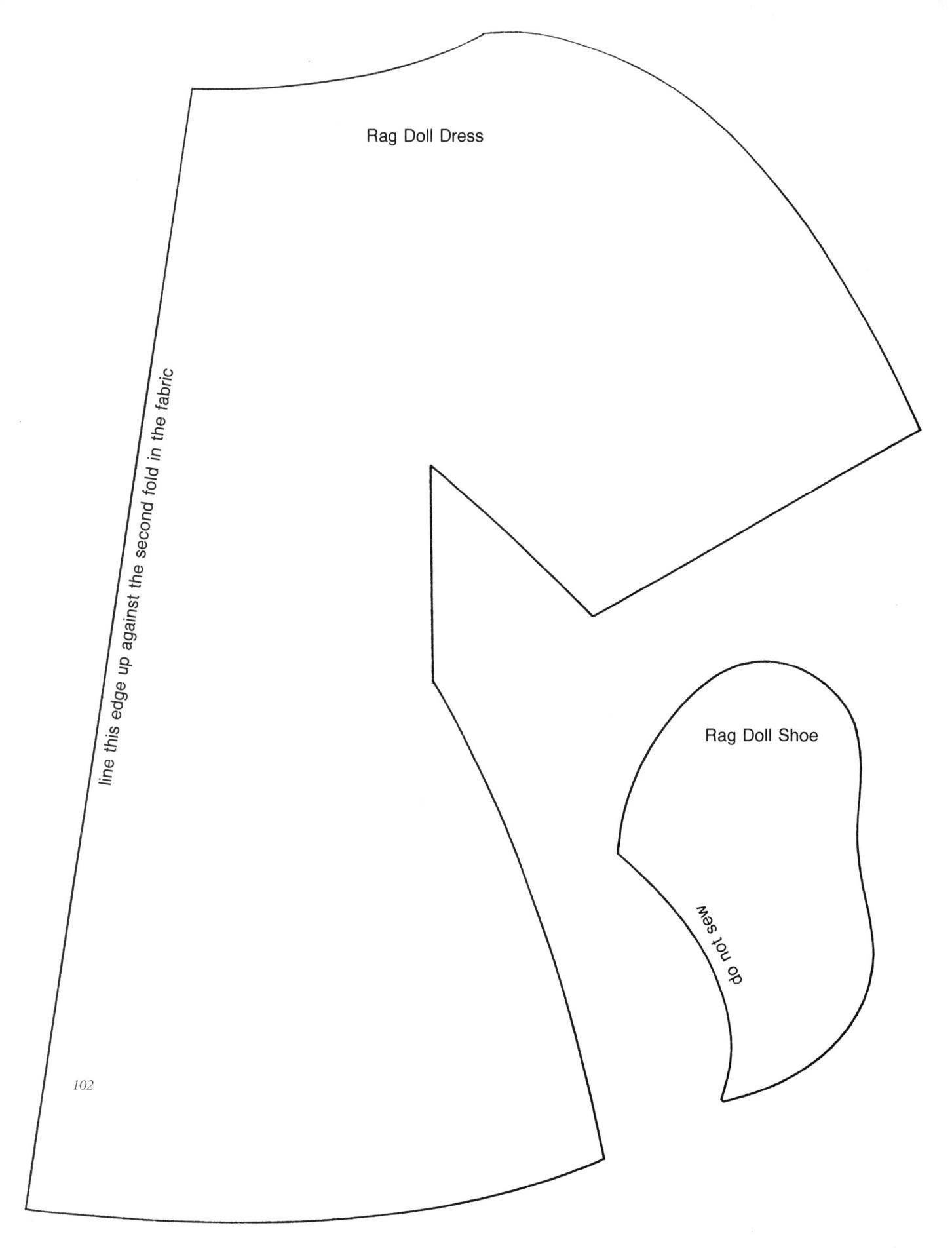

line this edge up against the second fold in the fabric

Rag Doll Shoe

do not sew

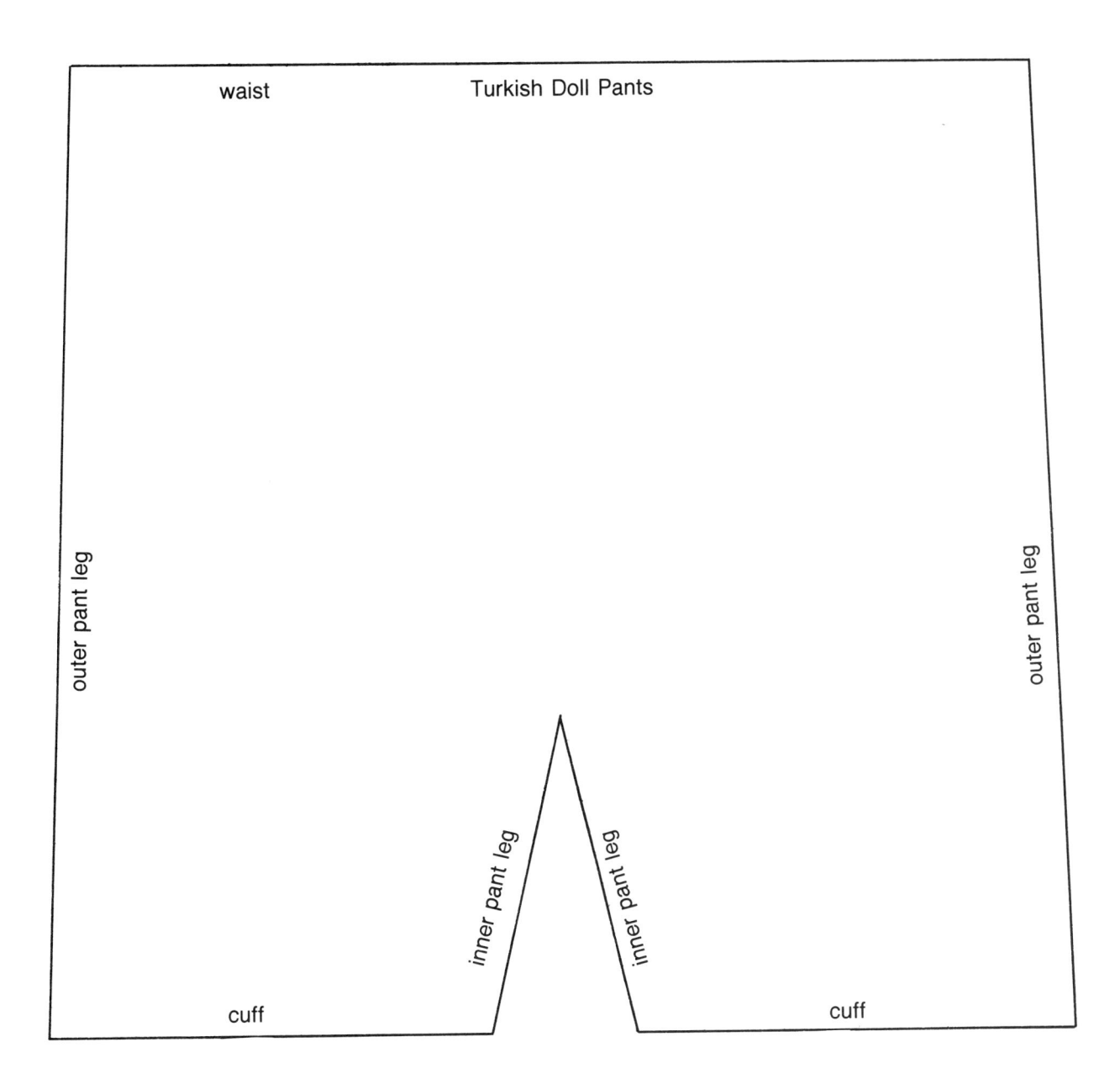

Turkish Doll Pants

waist

outer pant leg

outer pant leg

inner pant leg

inner pant leg

cuff

cuff

line this edge up against the fold in the fabric

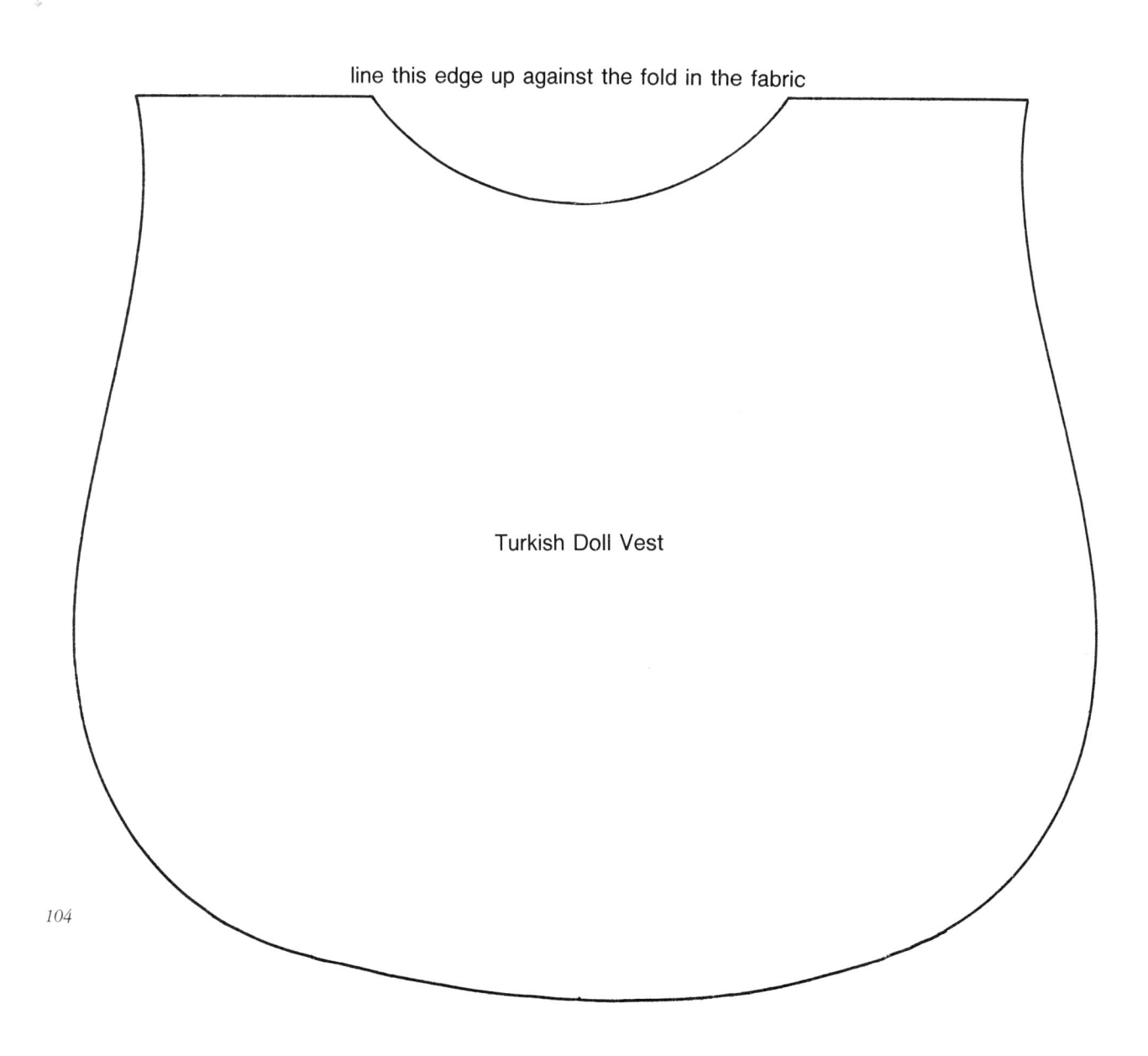

Turkish Doll Vest

top

Turkish Doll Fez

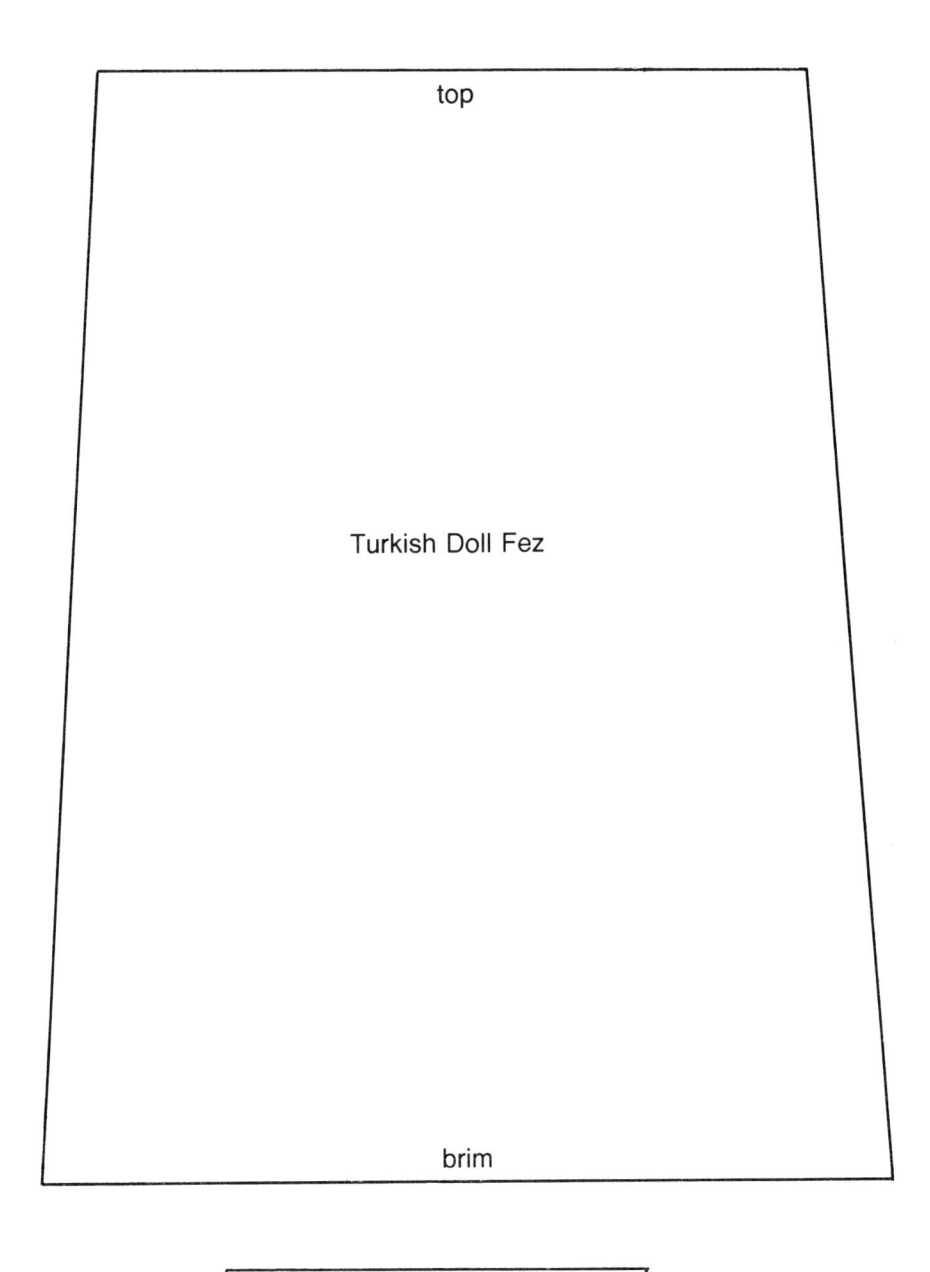

brim

do not sew

Turkish Doll Shoe

Iroquois Doll Shirt

line this edge up against the second fold in the fabric

Iroquois Doll Moccasins

do not sew

Iroquois Doll Pants

waist

outer pant leg

inner pant leg

inner pant leg

outer pant leg

cuff

cuff

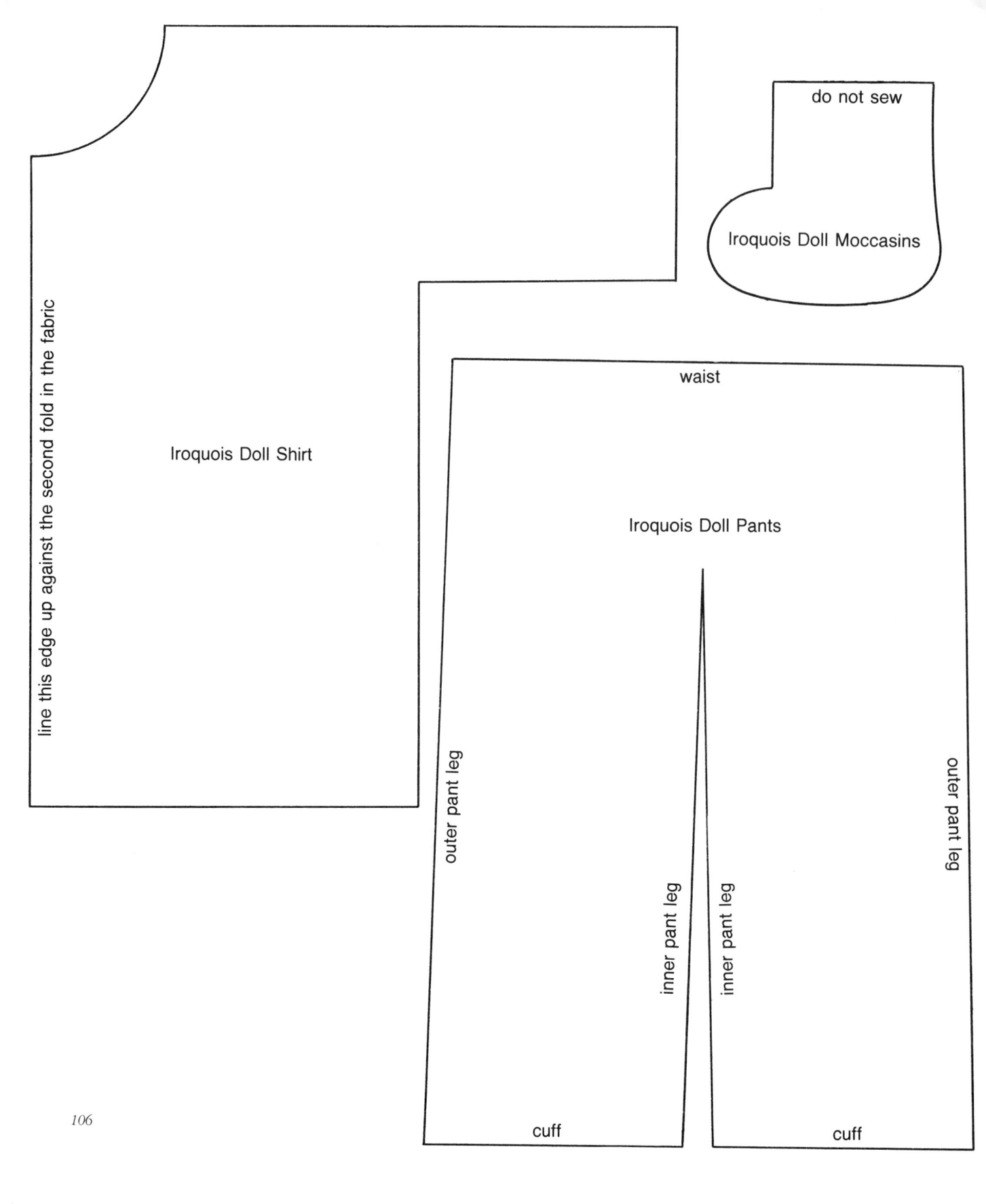

106

arm

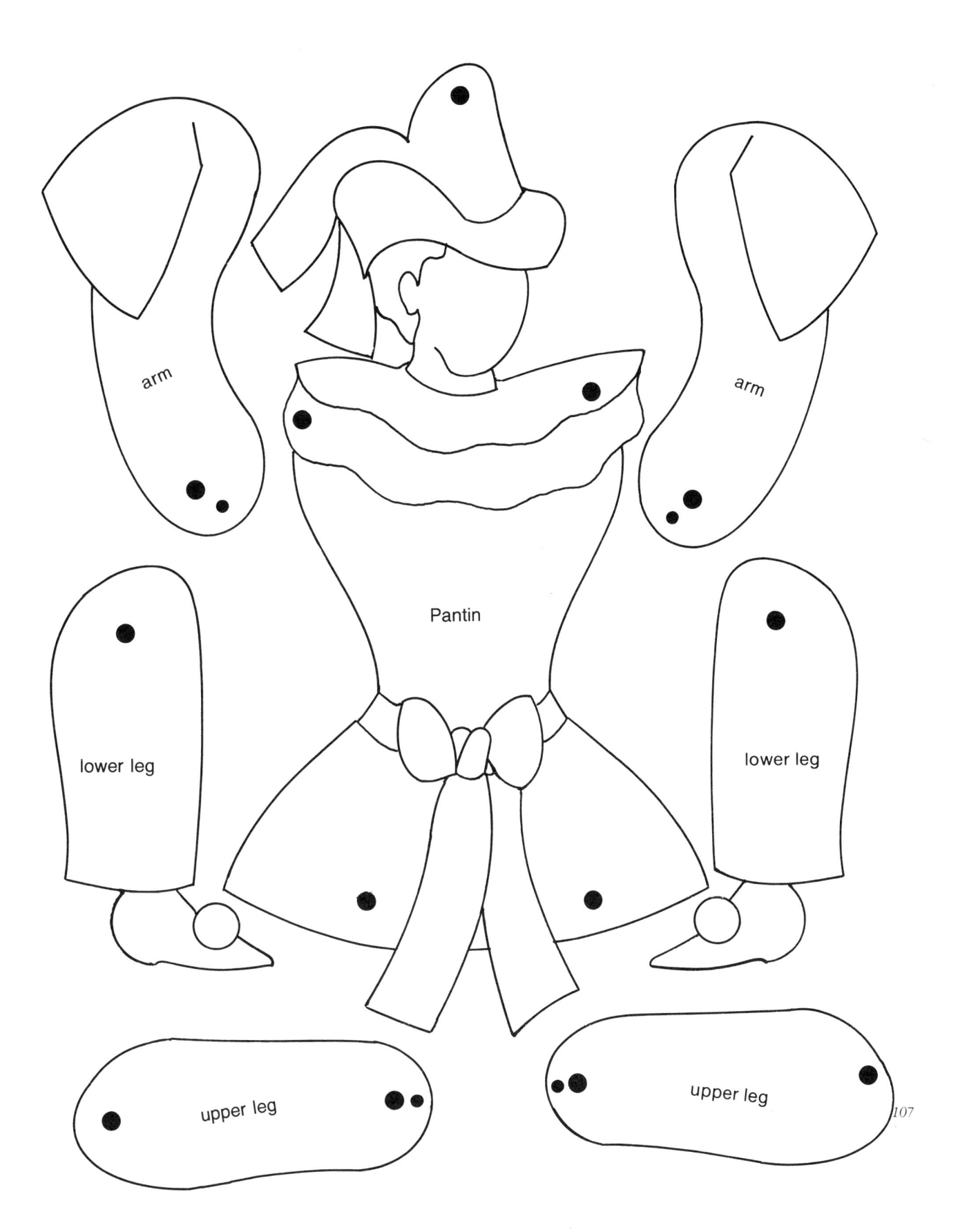

arm

Pantin

lower leg

lower leg

upper leg

upper leg

107

neckline

Peddler Cape

line this edge up against the fold in the fabric

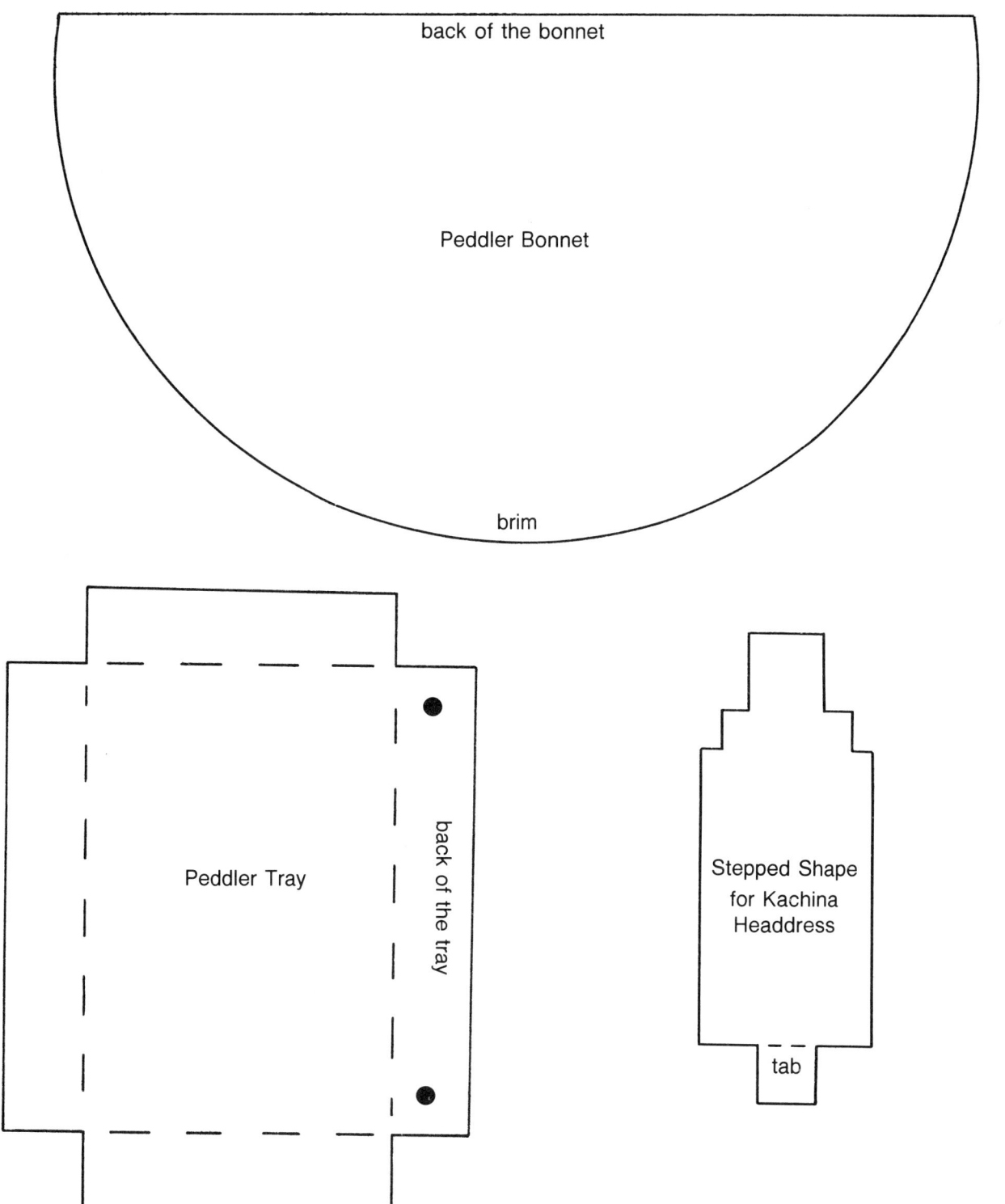

back of the bonnet

Peddler Bonnet

brim

Peddler Tray

back of the tray

Stepped Shape for Kachina Headdress

tab

Sudanese Doll

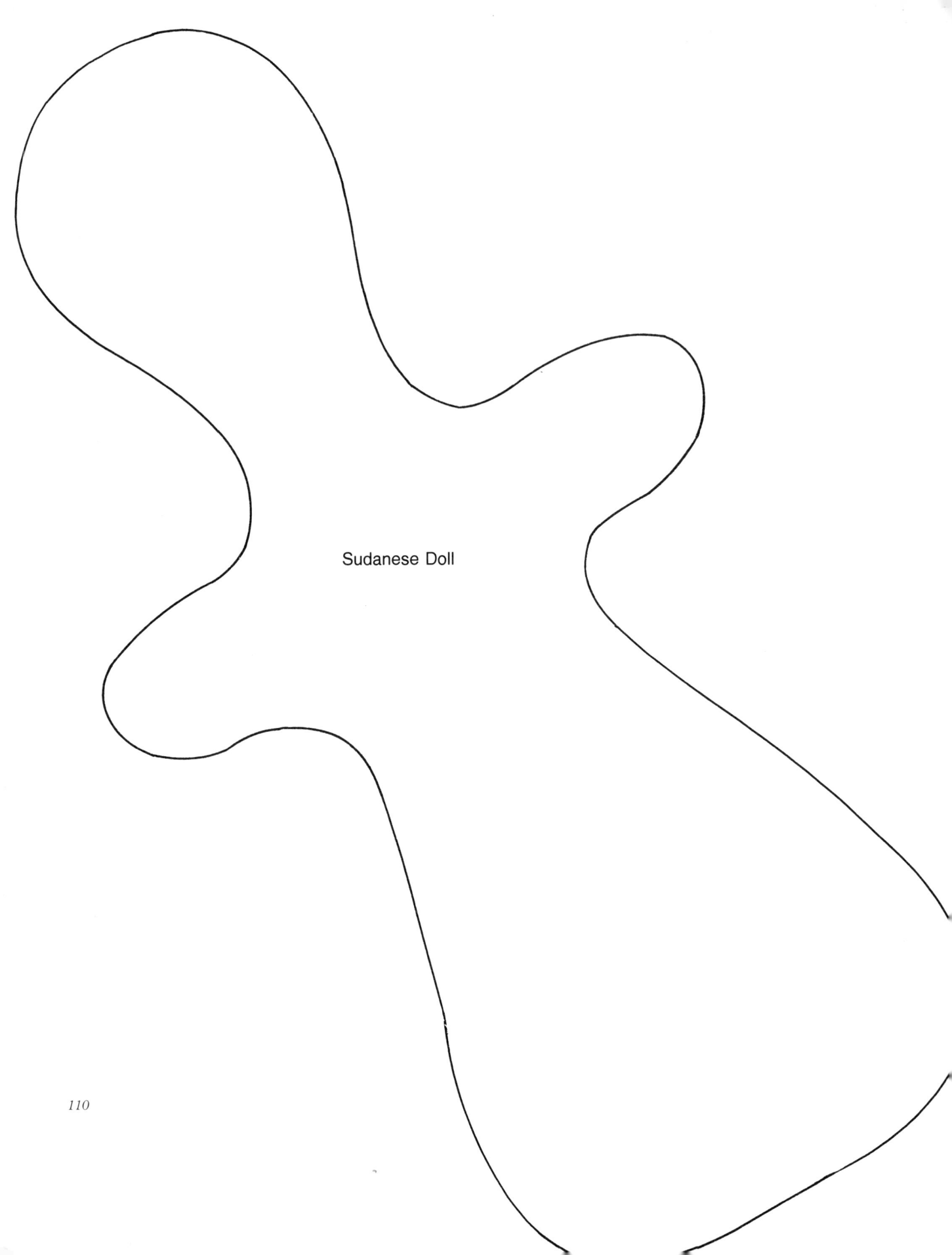

Sudanese Doll Hat

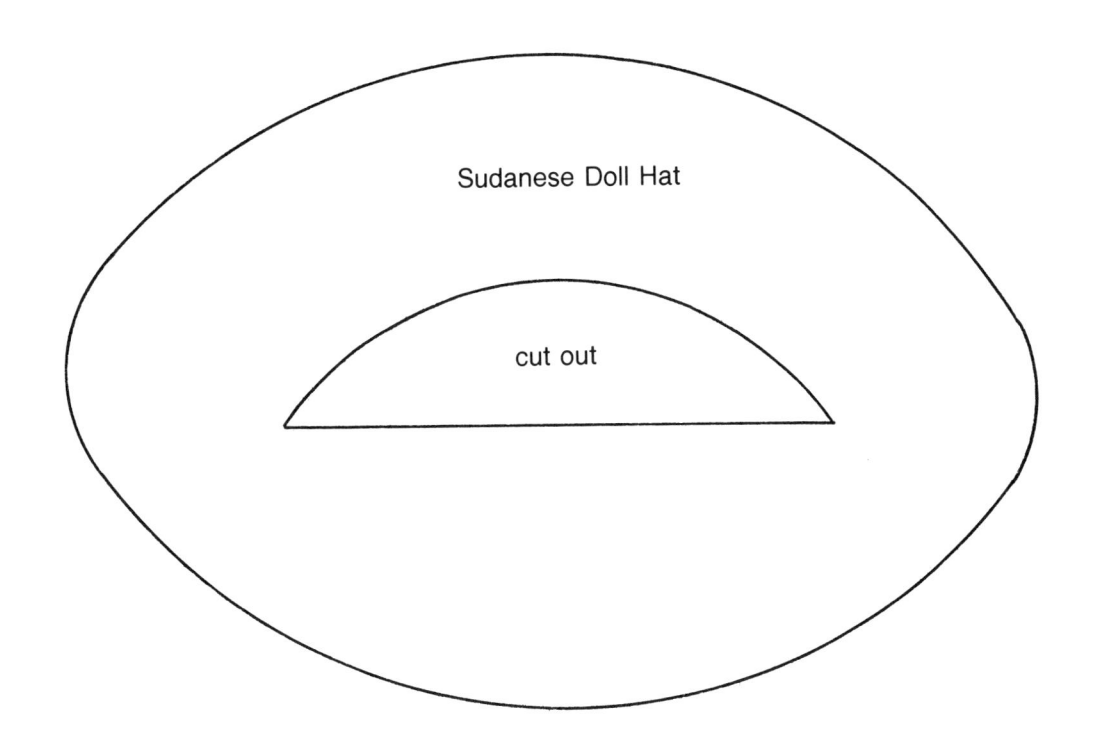

cut out

top

Fortune Teller Petal

bottom

Fortune Teller Blouse

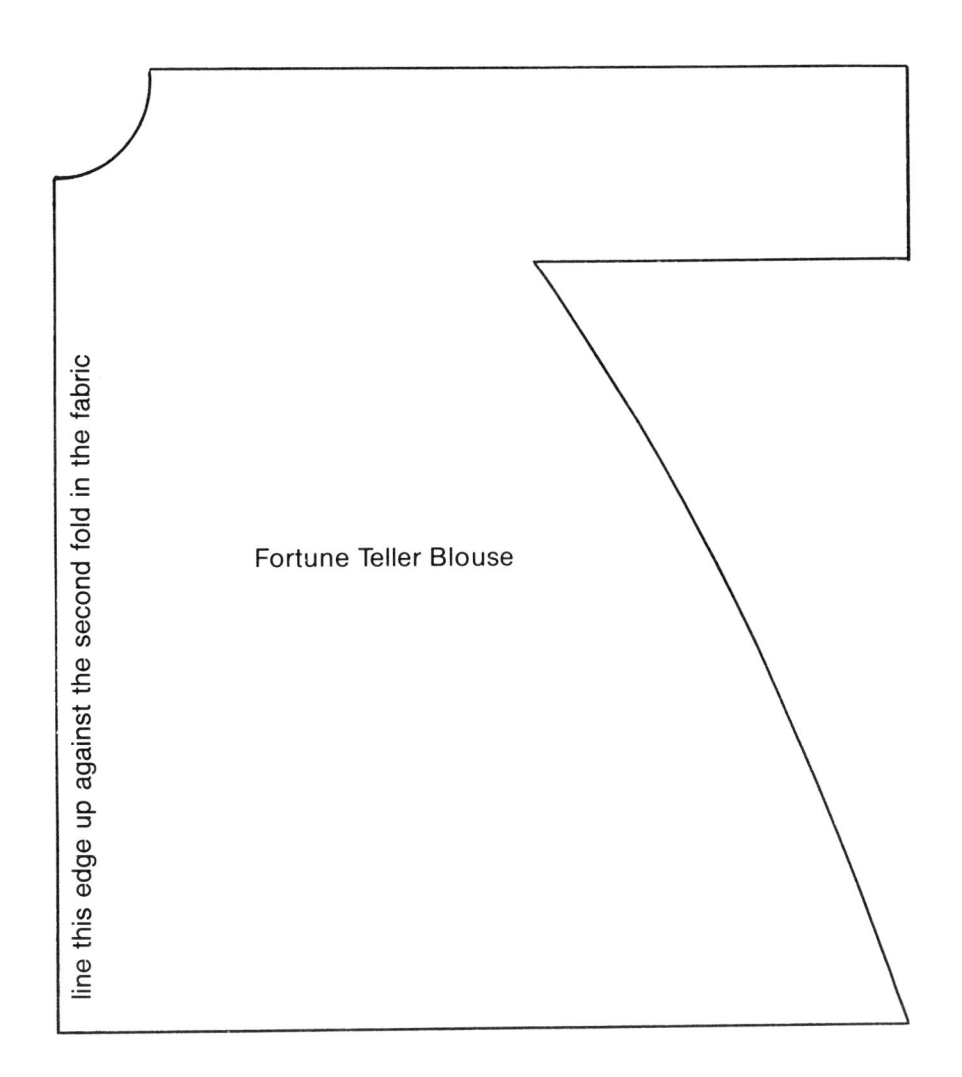

line this edge up against the second fold in the fabric